# The Liberation Manual

A guide to transcend the mirage of desires
and the illusion of mind.

**Venerable Ananda**

**The Liberation Manual**

First Print 2024



ISBN: 978-1-0369-0057-1

www.venerableananda.org

# Foreword

It is with immense joy and deep respect that I present the preface to **The Liberation Manual**, an extraordinary guide to the spiritual path authored by Venerable Panadure Ananda Thera, a revered Theravada Buddhist meditation master and monk. This book is not merely about Buddhism; it **is** Buddhism—a distilled, practical guide to the profound teachings of the Sutta Pitaka, brought to life through the clarity and wisdom of Venerable Ananda Thera.

Drawing inspiration from the insightful explanations of the late Most Venerable Katukurunde Ñāṇananda Maha Thera and Most Venerable Dankande Dhammaratana Maha Thera, this manual offers a direct path to overcoming any form of suffering or stress in this very moment. It is designed not only for those who are new to the spiritual journey but also for seasoned practitioners seeking to deepen their understanding and practice. True to its title, The Liberation Manual is concise, profound, and devoid of unnecessary complexities. It is a precious resource that cuts through the maze of conceptual distractions, presenting the essence of the Buddha's teachings in a manner that is both accessible and transformative.

One of the book's remarkable features is its detailed exposition of both insight meditation (vipassanā) and tranquilizing meditation (samatha). These techniques are meticulously described with a clear structure—starting, middle, and end—guiding the reader through each stage of practice. Venerable Ananda Thera skilfully illustrates how these meditative practices, when properly cultivated, lead to higher levels of spiritual awakening and profound inner peace. The clarity and precision with which these methods are presented make this manual an invaluable resource for practitioners at all levels, providing them with the tools needed to cultivate mindfulness, concentration, and ultimately, liberating wisdom.

In these pages, readers will find practical insights that illuminate the path to liberation, emphasizing the lived experience of freedom from mental constructs, desires, and the illusion of self. Venerable Ananda there masterfully guides us to see beyond the superficial layers of existence and recognize the underlying truths that lead to genuine liberation.

This manual serves as a beacon for all who are genuinely committed to understanding the nature of reality and walking the path of Dhamma. It is not just a book to be read, but a guide to be lived, offering practical wisdom to help navigate the challenges of modern life with serenity and insight.

I wholeheartedly commend **The Liberation Manual** to all seekers of truth, whether they are just beginning their journey or have been walking the path for years. It is a remarkable contribution to the spiritual literature of our time, and I am confident that it will serve as a guiding light for many on the road to awakening.

May this work be a source of wisdom and inspiration to all who read it. May it lead to the realization of true peace and liberation.

Most Venerable Induragare Dhammarathana Maha Thera,
Theravada Buddhist Monk,
Senior Professor,
Department of Sanskrit and Eastern studies,
University of Kelaniya,
Sri Lanka.

# Preface

It is with great joy and a deep sense of responsibility that I present this book to you, a concise yet comprehensive guide on the path to liberation. This book was inspired by my foreign meditation students, who invited me to write something that could distill the essential knowledge needed to understand the reality of life and the path to true freedom. The goal of this book is simple: to provide you with the wisdom and practical meditation techniques necessary to transcend suffering and attain Nibbāna—enlightenment—in this very life.

Unlike many other texts, this book does not focus solely on theories and intellectual discourse. While theory is important, it is the practical aspect of meditation that truly transforms one's experience and understanding of life. Many books discuss meditation, but few truly teach it in a way that is accessible, clear, and results-oriented. My intention here is to offer a step-by-step guide, blending the profound teachings of Buddhism with the practical methods that I have personally used to guide thousands of students—both local and foreign—toward liberation.

I ask that as you read this book, you set aside any preconceived notions or knowledge you may have heard or learned before. Approach it as a beginner, without any fixed ideas or mental frames. Whether you are completely new to Buddhism and meditation, or someone who has already explored these topics, I invite you to engage with this book with fresh eyes and an open heart. You may find that the truths discussed here are simpler than you think, and that the path to Nibbāna is not as distant as many believe. In fact, after reading this book, you will come to understand that liberation is here and now, attainable through dedicated practice.

This book is a distillation of essential concepts, including the reality of life, the nature of desires, the Four Noble Truths, the root of ignorance, and many other teachings that help develop wisdom. Additionally, it provides meditation techniques from both the Samatha (tranquilizing) and Vipassanā (insight) traditions. The culmination of this journey is Nibbāna, the ultimate liberation, and my goal is for you to realize that this is not something far away but something within reach, right here in this very moment.

To understand the source of this knowledge and the teachings within, let me share a little about myself—not out of ego, but to help you grasp how I have come to these realizations. I am a Theravāda Buddhist monk, and my life's work is devoted to guiding people toward liberation. But my journey did not begin in a Buddhist family. I was born into a Catholic household and was the only child. Like many children, I was full of desires and ambitions. I excelled academically and was always at the top of my class. I had big plans for my future—my ultimate goal was to become a High Court Justice.

However, one particular desire consumed me, a desire that would later change my life entirely. I had a deep yearning for the presence of an elder sister, someone who could be a loving, nurturing figure like a mother. This desire was so strong that it became an obsession. It caused me immense suffering, but as an introvert, I kept these emotions hidden. To the outside world, I appeared as a serious, focused, and professional individual, but inside, I was constantly plagued by this unfulfilled longing.

I prayed to God frequently and turned to the Bible for solace. At the same time, I found myself drawn to meditation books, particularly in search of methods to attain supernatural powers. It was through this exploration that I came across Buddhist teachings and meditation practices, which sparked a profound transformation in my life. I realized that desires are like a mirage—they promise satisfaction but only lead to more suffering. The only way to be free from suffering is to relinquish all phenomena and still the physical, verbal, and mental formations that keep us trapped.

This book is, in many ways, a personal reflection of the path I took to overcome my own suffering. It contains the step-by-step guidance I followed to attain peace, joy, and ultimately liberation. At the age of 13, I made the decision to convert to Buddhism on my own, despite being raised in a Catholic family. By the age of 15, I was ordained as a Buddhist monk, having left my home forcefully in search of deeper truths. During this time, I immersed myself in the study of the Tipiṭaka (the Buddhist scriptures), with a particular focus on the Sutta Piṭaka. These ancient texts were my guide as I embarked on this spiritual journey, and they form the foundation of the teachings presented in this book.

In pursuit of higher meditation practices, I later traveled to a renowned meditation monastery in Myanmar, where I lived for several years. There, I deepened my meditation practice and gained further insights into the teachings of the Lord Buddha. While the knowledge I gained through reading and study was invaluable, it was through meditation and direct experience that I truly understood the path to liberation. This is the method I teach to my students, and it is what I offer you through the pages of this book.

Ultimately, this book is not just a collection of teachings—it is a practical manual for those who are serious about attaining liberation from suffering. My hope is that as you read, you will not only gain intellectual understanding but also be inspired to put these teachings into practice in your own life. The path to Nibbāna is real and achievable, and it begins with the willingness to let go of all that binds us to suffering.

I bless you all with the strength and determination to walk this path. May you find peace, joy, and liberation in this very life. The way to live beyond suffering is here, and I invite you to walk it with me.

May you be well, may you be happy, and may you be liberated!

With Boundless Metta,
Venerable Panadure Ananda Thero,
A Buddhist Meditation Master.

# Introduction

Welcome to a transformative journey toward liberation, a journey that transcends the illusions of desire and suffering to unveil the profound peace that lies within. In these pages, I invite you to explore the essential teachings of Buddhism, rooted in the timeless wisdom of the Lord Buddha, and discover practical meditation techniques that can lead you to enlightenment—Nibbāna—in this very life.

In a world filled with distractions and desires, we often find ourselves chasing after fleeting pleasures, mistaking them for true happiness. Yet, as you will discover in the first chapter, *"The Mirage of Desire: Why True Liberation is the Only Path to Lasting Peace,"* these desires are mere illusions that can never satisfy our deeper yearning for peace. This book aims to challenge these misconceptions and guide you toward understanding that true liberation is attainable through mindful living and meditation.

**Understanding the Nature of Suffering**

Throughout our lives, we encounter various forms of suffering, whether emotional, physical, or existential. *"The Medicine to Overcome Any Kind of Suffering/Stress: Understanding the Nature of Anatta/Non-Self/No Soul"* dives deep into the fundamental Buddhist concept of Anatta, or non-self, revealing how our attachments and identifications with the self contribute to our suffering. By understanding that the self is an illusion, we can begin to disentangle ourselves from the grip of our desires and fears, allowing for a profound shift in our experience of life.

### The Power of the Present Moment

Central to the teachings within this book is the transformative power of living fully in the present moment. In *"The Power of Now: Living Fully in the Present Moment,"* you will learn that true happiness is not found in the past or future but is available to us right now. This chapter emphasizes mindfulness as a crucial practice that anchors us in the present, enabling us to experience life more fully and with greater clarity.

As we journey through the chapters, we will also confront the veil of ignorance that clouds our perception of reality, perpetuating our suffering. Understanding the nature of stress and suffering is essential, and in *"The Ultimate Truth of Life: Understanding and Transcending Stress and Suffering,"* we will examine how cravings and misunderstandings lead to a cycle of dissatisfaction. By recognizing these patterns, you can begin to cultivate awareness that liberates you from the cycles of suffering.

### The Interconnectedness of Existence

The book also explores profound concepts such as Dependent Origination (Paṭicca Samuppāda) in *"The Heart of Buddhism: Dependent Origination."* This principle teaches us about the interconnectedness of all phenomena, shedding light on how our thoughts, actions, and intentions create a ripple effect in our lives and the world around us. By understanding this intricate web, we can take responsibility for our experiences and work toward positive change.

**Practical Steps to Liberation**

You will also find detailed meditation techniques designed to cultivate mindfulness and insight, such as the *"16 Steps of Anapanasati: A Comprehensive Guide to Breath Meditation."* Each technique is a pathway to stilling the mind, discerning impermanence, and relinquishing attachments that bind us to suffering. Chapters like *"The First Step to Liberation: Penetrative Attention (Yoniso Manasikāra)"* provide practical, actionable steps that you can integrate into your daily life, allowing for a gradual yet profound transformation.

As you progress through the book, *"The Four Stages of Liberation: From Stream-Entry to Full Enlightenment,"* will guide you through the stages of awakening. Understanding these stages allows you to recognize your own journey toward liberation, helping you navigate the challenges and milestones along the way.

## A Personal Invitation

Ultimately, this book is more than just a collection of teachings; it is a practical manual for anyone serious about walking the path to liberation. Whether you are a beginner seeking clarity or an experienced practitioner looking to deepen your practice, you will find guidance and inspiration within these pages. My intention is not only to impart knowledge but to encourage you to engage deeply with these teachings and apply them to your own life.

I encourage you to approach this text with an open heart and mind, free from preconceived notions. Let this journey lead you to insights that can transform your understanding of life, the nature of suffering, and the profound joy that comes from liberation.

## A Journey Together

As you embark on this journey, I invite you to walk alongside me. The teachings presented here are not just theoretical; they are grounded in my own experiences and the many paths I have witnessed in my students. The essence of this book lies in its practicality and accessibility, aiming to empower you to take your first steps or deepen your practice on the path to Nibbāna.

May your exploration of these teachings bring you closer to the peace and freedom that lie at the heart of existence.

With boundless metta,
Venerable Panadure Ananda Thero,
A Buddhist Meditation Master

# Contents

***"Apârutâ tesam amatassa dvârâ***
***Ye sotavanto pamuñcantu saddham"***

"The doors to the Deathless have been opened for you. Those who have ears, let them hear with faith and be liberated."

# 1
# The Mirage of Desire:
## *Why True Liberation is the Only Path to Lasting Peace*

In our daily lives, we constantly chase after desires, believing that the next achievement or possession will bring us lasting happiness. Desires are like a mirage in the desert: from a distance, they appear to promise something exquisite, something that will finally fulfil us. But as we get closer and attain what we longed for, the promised satisfaction slips through our fingers, leaving us just as thirsty as before.

Take, for example, the pursuit of wealth. Many people believe that if they can just earn enough money, they will finally be at peace. But once they achieve their financial goals, they often find that the satisfaction is fleeting. Soon, new desires emerge—perhaps for more wealth, more possessions, or new experiences. The cycle begins again, and no matter how much is accumulated, true peace remains elusive.

This cycle isn't limited to material wealth. It's the same with relationships, status, or any form of sensual pleasure. A person might think that finding the perfect partner will complete them. However, even the most fulfilling relationships can become a source of stress and dissatisfaction if they are rooted in the endless pursuit of desire.

Imagine a dog chasing its tail. It runs in circles, convinced that if it can just catch its tail, it will have what it wants. But even if it does catch its tail, what has it really achieved? The satisfaction is momentary, and soon the chase begins anew. In a similar way, we chase our desires, not realizing that the act of chasing is what creates our dissatisfaction.

Even more telling is the story of the dog licking a bloody bone. The dog, driven by hunger, licks the bone with fervour, thinking it is gaining nourishment. In reality, the bone is dry, and the blood it tastes is its own, from the wounds caused by its desperate licking. This is what happens when we pursue desires with the belief that they will satisfy us—we end up hurting ourselves, draining our own energy, and feeding on our own suffering.

The truth is that desires are self-generated. Our minds create thoughts and perceptions, and these give rise to sensations that we then experience as pleasure or pain. But these sensations are merely echoes of our own thoughts, and chasing them is like trying to hold on to the wind. No matter how hard we try, they slip away, leaving us restless and exhausted.

Real peace, real satisfaction, comes not from fulfilling desires but from emptying the mind of them. When the mind is free of the ripples caused by endless desires and expectations, it can settle into a state of true calm. This is the state of liberation, where the mind is no longer driven by the illusion that something outside of itself can bring lasting happiness.

To truly experience the ecstasy of life, to find real and enduring satisfaction, we must liberate ourselves from the illusion of desire. This liberation is not about giving up pleasure or becoming detached from life; rather, it is about seeing through the mirage of desire and understanding that the peace we seek is already within us, waiting to be uncovered.

In this way, liberation becomes the only path to lasting peace, because it frees us from the endless cycle of chasing after what can never truly satisfy. It allows us to rest in the fullness of life as it is, without the constant need to seek something more.

# 2

# The Power of Now:

## *Living Fully in the Present Moment*

In our fast-paced world, we often find ourselves caught up in the rush of daily life, constantly thinking ahead or reflecting on the past. We plan, we worry, we analyse, and we ruminate, but in doing so, we overlook the simple truth that life is unfolding right here, right now. This constant mental activity pulls us away from the present moment, causing us to miss out on the richness of life that can only be experienced when we live fully and intensely in the present.

Imagine you're drinking a cup of coffee. Instead of savouring the warmth of the cup in your hands, the aroma of the coffee, and the taste as it touches your lips, your mind is elsewhere. You're thinking about your to-do list, replaying a conversation from yesterday, or worrying about tomorrow's meeting. The simple pleasure of drinking coffee is overshadowed by a stream of thoughts, and as a result, you miss out on truly experiencing the moment.

Consider the lives of two men, each at opposite ends of the socio-economic spectrum. The first man is poor, homeless, and living under a tree. Despite his circumstances, he sits down to drink a cup of tea from a broken mug. As he does, he is fully present, completely immersed in the moment. He notices the warmth of the tea, the rustling of the leaves above him, the gentle breeze on his skin. There are no distractions in his mind; he is living fully in this moment, and in doing so, he experiences a deep sense of contentment.

The second man, by contrast, is wealthy beyond imagination. He is being driven to his office in the back seat of a Rolls-Royce Phantom, sipping champagne from a crystal glass. But despite the luxury that surrounds him, his mind is elsewhere. He is thinking about how others perceive him, worrying about his family and business, and grappling with his ego. His thoughts are a whirlwind, pulling him in a thousand directions, preventing him from enjoying the present moment. Despite his wealth, he is not truly living; he is merely existing, lost in a maze of thoughts.

So, who is truly happy? The poor man, who lives fully in the present moment, or the rich man, whose mind is consumed by thoughts? The answer is clear: true happiness does not come from wealth or status, but from the ability to be present. The poor man, though lacking in material possessions, finds joy in the simple act of living in the now. The rich man, though surrounded by luxury, is a prisoner of his own mind, unable to experience the moment.

Life is like a river, constantly flowing and changing. Just as you cannot step into the same river twice, you cannot experience the same moment twice. The water you touched a moment ago has already flowed downstream, and new water has taken its place. If you are thinking about the water that has already passed, you miss the water that is flowing by now. In the same way, if you are thinking about the past or the future, you miss the present moment, which is the only moment that truly exists.

The past and future are mere illusions, constructs of the mind that arise as thoughts in the present. You cannot go back to the past, nor can you leap forward into the future, even for a single second. All you have is the present moment, and yet we spend so much of our lives missing it, caught up in thoughts about what was or what might be.

When the mind is empty of thoughts, there are no worries, no desires, no fears—only peace. The rich man, too, could experience this peace if he learned to drop his thoughts and be present. The key to a happy life is not in accumulating wealth or status, but in cultivating the ability to live fully in the now. When we let go of our thoughts and immerse ourselves in the present moment, we discover the true ecstasy of life—a sense of satisfaction that no amount of wealth or success can bring.

To live completely and intensely in this very moment is to embrace life as it is, without clinging to the past or yearning for the future. It is to find joy in the simple act of being, in the awareness that life is happening now, and that now is all there is.

# 3

# The Medicine to Overcome Any Kind of Suffering/Stress:

## *Understanding the Nature of Anatta/Non-Self/No Soul*

In our quest to overcome suffering and stress, we often look for external solutions or practices that promise relief. However, according to Buddhist teachings, the ultimate medicine for any form of suffering lies in understanding the nature of anatta, or non-self. This concept challenges our deepest beliefs about identity and existence, revealing that our struggle with suffering is rooted in a fundamental misunderstanding of our own nature.

### The Illusion of the Self

Human beings across cultures and religions have different approaches to the idea of the soul. In many belief systems, there is a quest to either preserve the soul in a heavenly realm or to dissolve it through various practices.

However, Buddhism offers a unique perspective: true liberation comes not from trying to permanently preserve or dissolve the soul, but from realizing that there is no permanent, unchanging self to begin with.

Imagine life as a sophisticated robot programmed with artificial intelligence. This robot has sensors to see, hear, and feel, and it can process information through its programming. Yet, despite its abilities, it has no soul—no inherent, permanent self. It operates purely through a set of mechanisms and responses. Its existence is defined by causes and effects, not by an intrinsic essence.

Our human minds are similarly programmed with concepts of self. We have ingrained ideas about the nature of our existence, which can be summarized into 20 aspects related to our body, sensations, perceptions, volitional activities, and cognitions. Here are a few examples of these concepts:

1. Body is my soul: The belief that our physical body is the essence of our self.
2. My soul is associated with my body: The idea that a separate soul is linked to our physical form.
3. My soul is inside my body: The notion that the soul resides within our body, distinct from it.
4. My body is not my soul, but something else is my soul: The idea that the soul is something separate from the body, applied similarly to sensations, perceptions, volitional activities, and cognitions.

These concepts are like software programmed into our minds, shaping how we perceive ourselves and our experiences. Just as a robot can only function with its programming, our understanding of self and existence is governed by these ingrained concepts.

**The Duality of Experience**

When we experience the world, our cognition processes inputs from our senses. However, this experience is coloured by our programmed understanding of duality: the distinction between "the thing experienced" and "the one who experiences." This dualistic view creates a sense of separation and contributes to the illusion of self.

In Buddhism, this illusion of duality is known as avijja or ignorance. It is the fundamental misperception that creates a false sense of self and leads to suffering. Just as a robot does not know it is a machine, humans do not realize that their sense of self is an illusion. We mistakenly believe that there is a permanent, unchanging self that experiences and suffers.

**Liberation Through Understanding**

If the robot were to gain awareness that it is merely a machine, it would cease to be troubled by its functions and limitations. Similarly, when we understand that our sense of self is an illusion created by our thoughts and programming, we can liberate ourselves from the suffering caused by this illusion.

By ceasing to conceive of ourselves as separate and distinct entities—by stopping the mental process that creates duality—we can overcome stress and suffering. This realization allows us to experience life as it is, free from the constraints of a self that is constantly seeking and desiring.

In practical terms, this means that when we stop clinging to the idea of a permanent self and recognize the transient nature of our thoughts and experiences, we can achieve true liberation. Our suffering and stress are not caused by external factors but by our own misconceptions about the self. By understanding and letting go of these misconceptions, we find freedom from the cycles of craving and dissatisfaction.

Understanding the nature of anatta or non-self is not just an abstract philosophical idea but a practical tool for overcoming suffering. By recognizing that our perceived self is an illusion, we can transcend the cycle of desire and aversion that causes our distress. This realization brings about a profound shift in our experience, allowing us to live with greater peace and contentment.

# 4
# The Ultimate Truth of Life:
## *Understanding and Transcending Stress and Suffering*

When contemplating the ultimate truth of life, many might be surprised to find that the core of existence often reveals itself through stress and suffering. Despite our relentless pursuit of happiness through various physical, verbal, and mental activities, the ultimate truth may seem to be that these efforts often culminate in just another layer of stress and fatigue.

**The Nature of Existence**

Our lives are filled with a multitude of activities—work, relationships, hobbies, and pursuits of pleasure—all driven by the desire to find joy and fulfilment. However, these pursuits, when examined deeply, often lead to a state of stress and restlessness. The pleasure we experience is frequently self-generated, a by-product of our own thought patterns and mental constructs. This pleasure is fleeting, and once the immediate satisfaction fades, we are left with the same underlying stress and fatigue.

**The cause of Suffering**

Craving is the root cause of much of our suffering. We crave not only physical pleasure but also engage in verbal and mental activities in the hope of finding happiness. For instance, consider the aftermath of a social event—a party or a deep conversation. The initial excitement and engagement may give way to exhaustion and stress, leaving us with a sense of emptiness once the event concludes. This cycle of craving, pursuit, and resultant fatigue is a stark reminder that the pleasure sought through these activities is often ephemeral.

**Understanding the Cessation of Suffering**

The way to truly address suffering is not by engaging more intensely in physical, verbal, or mental activities but by understanding the root cause of our distress. According to Buddhist teachings, the cessation of suffering involves recognizing the nature of non-self (anatta) and the futility of seeking lasting happiness through external means.

1. Understanding Non-Self: By comprehending that there is no permanent, unchanging self, we can let go of the

craving that drives our suffering. This insight helps us realize that our sense of self is a construct, and by relinquishing attachment to this illusion, we can alleviate much of our stress.

2. Engaging in Enlightened Thoughts: Cultivating awareness and understanding through enlightened thoughts—such as the recognition of impermanence (anicca) and suffering (dukkha)—helps to maintain clarity and reduce the impact of craving.

3. Ethical Living: Adhering to ethical principles is crucial in the path to cessation of suffering. This includes avoiding harmful actions such as killing, stealing, sexual misconduct, lying, and the use of intoxicants. These ethical practices help in reducing the negative impact of our actions on ourselves and others.

4. Mindfulness and Awareness: Being mindful of our body, sensations, thoughts, and moods is essential. By observing these aspects of our experience without attachment or identification, we can maintain an understanding of the true nature of existence. Being a witness rather than a participant in our mental and physical processes helps prevent falling into the delusion of a permanent self.

5. Cultivating Jhana and Contemplation: Through meditation practices, such as the development of jhana (deep states of concentration), we can experience a

profound cessation of stress. These practices support the understanding of the ultimate truth by allowing the mind to reach states of profound stillness and clarity.

## The Noble Eightfold Path

The culmination of these practices is found in the Noble Eightfold Path, which provides a comprehensive framework for transcending suffering. This path consists of:

1. Right Understanding: Comprehending the Four Noble Truths and the nature of suffering.
2. Right Intention: Cultivating intentions of renunciation, non-ill will, and compassion.
3. Right Speech: Engaging in truthful, kind, and beneficial communication.
4. Right Action: Acting ethically and refraining from harm.
5. Right Livelihood: Choosing a livelihood that does not cause harm or suffering to others.
6. Right Effort: Developing a diligent effort to cultivate wholesome states and abandon unwholesome states.
7. Right Mindfulness: Practicing mindfulness in all aspects of life to maintain awareness and insight.
8. Right Concentration: Engaging in meditation practices to develop deep states of concentration and insight.

## Conclusion

The Medicine to Overcome Any Kind of Suffering/Stress:

The ultimate truth of life is not found through relentless pursuit of physical, verbal, or mental activities, which often lead to just more stress and fatigue. Instead, it lies in the profound understanding of non-self and the cessation of craving. By embracing the teachings of Buddhism, practicing ethical behaviour, cultivating mindfulness, and following the Noble Eightfold Path, we can achieve a state of liberation from suffering and discover the true essence of peace and contentment.

# 5
# The Veil of Ignorance:
## *How Misunderstanding Reality Perpetuates Suffering*

Ignorance, in its most profound sense, is the root cause of our suffering and discontentment. In the context of Buddhist philosophy, ignorance is not simply a lack of knowledge but a fundamental misunderstanding of the true nature of reality. It is the failure to comprehend the ultimate truths of life: the reality of suffering, the cause of suffering, the cessation of suffering, and the path that leads to the end of suffering. However, ignorance also manifests in a more subtle and pervasive way—through the mistaken belief in the independent existence of a "self" and a "world" outside of our immediate cognition.

### The Illusion of an Independent World and Self

One of the most practical and deceptive aspects of ignorance is the belief that there is a world and a self that exist independently of our awareness or cognition. We are fooled into thinking that the external world and the internal self are separate, independent entities that exist on their own, without any dependence on our cognition. This belief gives rise to the duality of "me" and "the world," "observer" and "the observed," "internal" and "external." However, this duality is nothing more than a mental construct, an illusion that arises only after a cognitive process has occurred.

To illustrate this, consider the simple act of hearing a sound. When you hear a sound, the cognition of that sound occurs first. Only afterward does your mind create the concepts of "the sound" and "the listener." These concepts, however, are just thoughts that arise in the mind after the cognitive process, not before. But ignorance leads us to believe that the sound and the person hearing it exist independently of the cognition. In reality, what is cognized is just that—a momentary cognition that arises and passes away.

**The Thought Experiment: The Wall Behind You**

Let's explore this further with a thought experiment. Imagine you are sitting in a room with a wall behind you. If someone were to ask you, "Is there a wall behind you?" you would likely say yes. If they then asked, "If you see it or not, is the wall behind you still existing?" you might again say yes. If they asked, "If you think about it or not, is the wall still there?" your answer would likely remain yes. Even if they asked, "If you are unconscious or not, is the wall still there?" you would probably still say yes. And finally, if they asked, "If you die or not, will the wall still be there?" you would likely affirm that it would be.

But here is the critical question: When you say that the wall exists whether you see it or not, is that statement a truth or merely a thought arising in your mind right now? When you recognize that it is just a thought, you begin to see how deeply ignorance has entrenched itself in your understanding of reality. The wall behind you is not an independently existing entity; it is a thought that arises when you bring it into cognition. When you are not directly perceiving it, the wall exists only as a thought in your mind.

**The World as We Experience It**

This realization has profound implications for how we understand the world. What we experience here and now is the world as it exists for us—this mechanism. When you think about your school, for instance, you are not recalling the actual physical school but merely a thought that arises and passes in your mind. The school you remember is not a real, independent place; it is a thought, an image in your mind. Ignorance, however, covers this understanding by making us believe that the school, the wall, and all other objects of our perception exist independently of our cognition.

**The Deception of Ignorance**

Ignorance deceives us by preventing us from seeing thoughts as just thoughts and imaginations as just imaginations. Instead, it convinces us that there is an independently existing world and self, separate from our cognition. This deception leads us to form attachments, cravings, desires, and aversions based on the mistaken belief that the world and self are real and permanent.

Consider another example: Suppose you are listening to a speech, but your attention drifts for a few minutes. When your attention returns, you might say, "The sound was there, and I was there, but I missed hearing it." However, the reality is that during the moments of inattentiveness, there was no sound or listener in your experience according to your mechanism. Your assertion that the sound and the listener were there, is merely a thought that arises in the present moment, not an actual reality.

**The Path to Liberation**

Understanding this fundamental aspect of ignorance is crucial for overcoming suffering. By recognizing that the world and self we believe in are merely mental constructs that arise after cognition, we can begin to dismantle the attachments and desires that bind us to the cycle of suffering. When we comprehend that what we experience here and now is all that exists for us, we can let go of the illusions that ignorance creates.

This realization allows us to overcome stress, suffering, cravings, attachments, hatred, ego, and all other forms of mental affliction. By seeing through the veil of ignorance, we can liberate ourselves from the false belief in an independent world and self, and instead, experience reality as it truly is—momentary, fleeting, and ultimately empty of inherent existence.

**Conclusion**

Ignorance is not just a lack of knowledge; it is a fundamental misunderstanding of reality that perpetuates suffering. By understanding the true nature of cognition and seeing thoughts as just thoughts, we can overcome the illusion of an independently existing world and self. This understanding is the key to liberation, freeing us from the cycle of suffering and leading us to a state of true peace and contentment.

# 6
# Quadrilateral Questions:
## *The Limitations of Conceptual Thought and the Emptiness of Existence*

During the time of the Lord Buddha, scholars and thinkers often engaged in deep philosophical inquiries, asking questions that sought to define the nature of reality, existence, and the world around them. Among these were a set of quadrilateral questions, which posed significant challenges to conventional thinking. One of the most notable of these inquiries centred around the nature of the world:

1. Is the world existing?
2. Isn't the world existing?
3. Does the world either exist or not exist?
4. Does the world neither exist nor not exist?

When these questions were presented to the Lord Buddha, he rejected them outright, stating that they were fundamentally flawed. To understand why these questions are invalid, we can explore the nature of cognition and existence, drawing on analogies and examples that illustrate the Lord Buddha's profound insight.

The Nature of Conceptual Thought: The Example of the Behind Wall

To grasp the limitations of these quadrilateral questions, let's return to the example of the wall behind you. When asked, "Is there a wall behind you?" your immediate response might be "yes." But as we delve deeper, we realize that the affirmation of the wall's existence is not a truth in the ultimate sense; rather, it is merely a thought, a concept that arises in your mind at that moment. This concept has no independent reality; it is simply a cognitive construct—a fleeting thought that appears and disappears within your mental landscape.

Now, if we consider the question, "Is there no wall behind you?" and you respond "no," this, too, is just another thought, a different conceptualization with no more inherent truth than the first. Similarly, when you entertain the questions of whether the wall "either exists or does not exist" or "neither exists nor does not exist," you are merely engaging with different configurations of thought—each arising and passing away without any substantial basis in reality.

The crux of the matter is that any statement about the existence or nonexistence of the wall (or the world) is simply data processed by your mental mechanism—much like a robot processing information. Whether the robot asserts that the world exists, does not exist, or falls into any of the other conceptual categories, these assertions are just data points generated by its programming. They have no intrinsic truth or reality beyond the moment of their arising.

**The Emptiness of Conceptualization: The Nature of the World**

This analogy extends to our understanding of the world itself. The quadrilateral questions about the world—whether it exists, does not exist, either, or neither—are similarly empty of intrinsic meaning. They are simply conceptual frameworks that arise within the mind, devoid of any inherent truth or reality. The Lord Buddha's rejection of these questions highlights the futility of trying to grasp the nature of reality through such binary and limited conceptual thinking.

In essence, the reality of the world is beyond these simplistic categories of thought. Just as the robot cannot make a meaningful statement about the existence or nonexistence of the world based on its limited programming, so too are we limited by our cognitive processes. Our minds, programmed by ignorance, generate these concepts, but they do not capture the true nature of reality.

**The Enlightened Perspective: Beyond Conceptual Thought**

An enlightened person, one who has transcended ignorance, understands that all conceptualizations are inherently empty. For such a person, the world is not something to be defined, categorized, or debated. The enlightened individual lives in a state of spontaneous awareness, free from the constraints of fixed ideas, beliefs, or judgments.

To the enlightened mind, the world is what is experienced in the present moment—nothing more, nothing less. There is no need to attach labels, form conclusions, or engage in speculative thought. The world is not something to be questioned in terms of existence or nonexistence; it simply is, as it is experienced right now.

This way of being is characterized by an emptied mindset—free from the constructs and limitations imposed by conceptual thought. It is a state of pure awareness, where the individual is fully present, living life completely and intensely, without the burden of mental frameworks. The enlightened person does not cling to any particular view, idea, or concept, because they have realized the emptiness of all such constructs.

**The Liberation from Mental Constructs**

The Lord Buddha's rejection of the quadrilateral questions serves as a profound teaching on the limitations of our conceptual minds. It encourages us to move beyond the intellectual pursuit of defining reality and instead to experience reality directly, without the filter of thoughts, labels, or judgments.

To live in such a way is to be liberated from the mental constructs that bind us to suffering. When we stop trying to define the world and instead experience it directly, we can free ourselves from the dualities that ignorance creates. We no longer need to ask whether the world exists or not, because we understand that such questions are merely products of a deluded mind.

In this state of liberation, we are no longer bound by the constraints of our cognitive programming. We live fully in the present moment, experiencing life as it unfolds, without the need for intellectualizing or categorizing our experiences. This is the essence of true freedom—freedom from the tyranny of conceptual thought and the limitations it imposes on our understanding of reality.

**Conclusion**

The quadrilateral questions that scholars posed to the Lord Buddha represent the limitations of conceptual thought in grasping the true nature of reality. The Lord Buddha's rejection of these questions serves as a powerful reminder that the ultimate truth lies beyond the confines of intellectual speculation. By understanding the emptiness of all conceptualizations, we can transcend the limitations of our cognitive processes and experience the world as it truly is—moment by moment, free from the delusions of existence and nonexistence. This is the path to true liberation, where we live fully and intensely in the present moment, with an emptied and awakened mind.

# 7
# The Root Sequence of All Phenomena: *Understanding Perception, Conception, and Liberation in the Mulapariyaya Sutta*

The Mulapariyaya Sutta, or the "Root Sequence Discourse," offers profound insights into the nature of perception, conception, and the path to liberation. It categorizes all objects and phenomena that can arise in the mind into 24 distinct categories, encompassing everything from the four primary elements to the abstract concepts of diversity, unity, and even Nibbāna, the ultimate liberation. Through this categorization, the sutta illustrates how ordinary people, trainees on the path to liberation, and fully liberated beings (Arahants and the Lord buddha) perceive and conceive these objects, revealing the deep-rooted mechanisms of ignorance and the potential for true liberation.

## The 24 Categories of Phenomena

The sutta categorizes all phenomena into 24 groups, beginning with the four primary elements:

1. The Four Elements: Earth (pathavi), water (apo), fire (tejo), and air (vayo), and the materials formed by their combinations.
2. Beings and Realms: Different beings in the universe and their respective planes of existence, from humans to the divine realms of devas and Brahma.
3. Arupa Jhanas: The dimensions of infinite space, infinite consciousness, infinite nothingness, and neither perception nor non-perception, representing the formless concentrations and the Brahma worlds of their practitioners.
4. Sense Data: The four classes of sense data—the seen, heard, sensed (smelling, tasting, and touching), and cognizance.
5. Abstract Concepts: The abstract categories of diversity, unity, and totality, or "The All."
6. Nibbāna: The ultimate liberation, characterized by the stilling of all formations and the cessation of existence.

## The Perception of an Ordinary Person

Let us begin with the first element, Patavi (earth element), and use a tangible example: a table. When an ordinary person perceives a table, they immediately conceive it as an independent, solid object existing in the world. This perception gives rise to a chain of thoughts and emotions—thoughts about the table, thoughts arising from the table, attachment to the table, and even happiness derived from the table. The mind, through ignorance, conceives the table as a permanent, self-existing entity that exists independently of the observer's cognition.

This erroneous conception is rooted in the ordinary person's misunderstanding of the true nature of phenomena. They believe that the table exists independently, whether they perceive it or not. This belief leads to the proliferation of thoughts and attachments, creating a web of mental formations that ultimately result in stress and suffering. The ordinary person’s perception is clouded by ignorance, leading them to take these mental formations as reality.

**The Perception of a Trainee on the Path to Liberation**

In contrast, when a trainee on the path to liberation perceives a table, their perception is accompanied by a special understanding. This understanding stems from their awareness of the true nature of phenomena—that all objects, including the table, do not exist independently but are merely cognitive constructs that arise and pass away in the mind. The trainee consciously refrains from conceiving the table as an independent entity.

By not conceiving the table as a self-existing object, the trainee prevents the arising of further thoughts and attachments. They recognize that the table is not a permanent, independent reality, but rather a temporary appearance in consciousness. This understanding weakens the proliferation of thoughts and diminishes the attachment and craving that typically follow the perception of an object. The trainee's perception is thus more aligned with the true nature of reality, reducing the stress and suffering associated with ignorance.

**The Perception of a Fully Liberated Being (Arahants and the Lord buddha)**

The fully enlightened being, such as an Arahant or the Lord buddha, perceives the table with complete understanding. For them, the table is perceived as it truly is—without any conception of it as an independent entity. Their perception is free from ignorance, and thus they do not generate thoughts about the table, from the table, or attachment to the table.

Because of this complete understanding, the fully liberated being experiences the table without the arising of any mental formations or attachments. They do not think of the table as "mine," nor do they derive happiness or suffering from its presence. The enlightened being's mind is free from the delusions that plague ordinary people, and thus they live in a state of pure awareness, unattached to any objects or phenomena.

**Understanding the Root Sequence of All Phenomena**

The Mulapariyaya Sutta describes how this process of perception and conception applies to all 24 categories of phenomena. Each category—from the four elements to the abstract concepts and even Nibbāna itself—can be perceived and conceived in different ways, depending on the level of understanding and liberation of the individual.

For the ordinary person, each category is perceived as an independent reality, leading to the proliferation of thoughts, attachments, and ultimately suffering. For the trainee, there is an effort to perceive these categories with special understanding, reducing the proliferation of thoughts and attachments. For the fully liberated being, these categories are perceived with complete understanding, free from any conception or attachment, leading to the cessation of suffering.

**The Path to Liberation**

By understanding this root sequence of all phenomena, one can begin to see how the mind creates its own suffering through the process of perception and conception. Ignorance causes us to conceive of the world as a collection of independent, self-existing entities, leading to attachment, craving, and suffering. But by recognizing the true nature of these phenomena as mere cognitive constructs, one can begin to unravel the web of ignorance and move towards liberation.

Liberation is achieved by fully understanding the nature of all phenomena, refraining from conceiving them as independent realities, and thereby preventing the arising of thoughts and attachments. This process culminates in the realization of Nibbāna, the stilling of all formations and the cessation of existence, where one is completely free from the cycle of birth, death, and suffering.

**Conclusion**

The Mulapariyaya Sutta offers a profound teaching on the nature of perception, conception, and liberation. By categorizing all phenomena into 24 groups and describing how they are perceived by ordinary people, trainees, and fully liberated beings, the sutta provides a roadmap for understanding the root sequence of all phenomena and the path to liberation. Through this understanding, one can transcend the limitations of ignorance, free the mind from the delusions of independent existence, and ultimately achieve the state of complete liberation.

# 8
# The Root of All Phenomena:
## *Understanding Desire, Attention, and Liberation in the Mulaka Sutta*

The Mulaka Sutta, or "The Root Discourse," provides a profound analysis of the fundamental principles that underlie all phenomena. It identifies the core elements that give rise to, sustain, and ultimately bring an end to all experiences. By understanding these principles, one can gain insight into the nature of reality and the path to liberation. The sutta outlines a sequence that begins with desire and culminates in Nibbāna, the cessation of all formations. This sequence serves as a roadmap for understanding how our experiences arise and how they can lead to either continued existence or liberation.

**1. All Phenomena Are Rooted in Desire**

Desire, or tanhā in Pali, is the fundamental root of all phenomena. It is the craving or longing that drives us to seek out and engage with experiences. Whether it is the desire for sensory pleasures, material possessions, or even spiritual attainments, this craving is the motivating force behind all of our actions and perceptions.

Imagine, for example, encountering a beautiful girl or a handsome boy. The root of your experience of their visual presence is desire. This desire propels you to focus on them, choosing this particular experience over others. It is the spark that ignites the entire chain of phenomena that follows.

**2. All Phenomena Come into Play Through Attention**

Attention (manasikāra) is the mechanism by which desire manifests. It is through attention that phenomena come into play in our consciousness. When we pay attention to an object, such as the sight of the beautiful girl or handsome boy, we allow it to occupy our mind, giving rise to a series of mental and physical reactions.

Attention directs our consciousness to specific objects, allowing the phenomena associated with them to arise. It is the lens through which our desires are channelled into concrete experiences.

**3. All Phenomena Have Contact as Their Origination**

Contact (phassa) is the origination of all phenomena. In the Buddhist framework, contact refers to the meeting point of the sense organ, the object, and consciousness. For example, when the eye sees the visual form of the girl or boy, this seeing, combined with visual cognition, results in contact.

This contact is the initial interaction that gives rise to the experience. It is the point at which the external world and internal consciousness intersect, leading to the arising of sensations, perceptions, and mental formations.

**4. All Phenomena Have Sensations as Their Meeting Place**

Sensations (vedanā) are the meeting place of all phenomena. Once contact has been established, it gives rise to sensations—feelings of pleasure, pain, or neutrality. These sensations are the immediate experiences that follow contact and are the foundation upon which further mental activities are built.

For instance, upon seeing the girl or boy, you might experience a pleasurable sensation. This sensation becomes the central meeting point of the experience, influencing how you perceive and respond to the visual object.

**5. All Phenomena Have Concentration as Their Presiding State**

Concentration (samādhi) is the presiding state of all phenomena. It is the mental factor that stabilizes and oversees the entire process, allowing the mind to remain focused on the object of attention. Concentration holds the experience together, ensuring that the mind remains immersed in the object of desire.

When you are fully absorbed in the visual experience of the girl or boy, concentration presides over the experience, maintaining your focus and allowing the experience to unfold without distraction.

**6. All Phenomena Have Mindfulness as Their Governing Principle**

Mindfulness (sati) is the governing principle of all phenomena. It is the mental faculty that controls and manages the experience, determining what should be the focus of attention and how it should be experienced. Mindfulness has the ability to regulate the flow of thoughts and can either allow them to proliferate or change the object of attention.

In the example of the girl or boy, mindfulness governs how you engage with the experience. It can choose to continue focusing on the visual form, create numerous thoughts about it, or shift the attention elsewhere.

**7. All Phenomena Have Discernment/Wisdom as Their Surpassing State**

Discernment or wisdom (paññā) is the surpassing state of all phenomena. It is the ability to see things as they truly are, beyond the surface level of appearances and desires. Wisdom discerns the impermanent, unsatisfactory, and non-self-nature of all phenomena, allowing one to transcend attachment and delusion.

Even in the midst of experiencing the visual of the girl or boy, wisdom can be applied to see through the illusion of independent existence and permanence. By discerning the true nature of the experience, one can begin to detach from it and overcome the delusion of self.

### 8. All Phenomena Have Liberation as Their Heartwood

Liberation (vimutti) is the heartwood or core of all experiences. It represents the ultimate goal of the Buddhist path—the release from the cycle of birth, death, and suffering. Liberation can be achieved through any experience when concentration, mindfulness, and wisdom are applied correctly.

Every experience, including the visual experience of the girl or boy, holds the potential for liberation. By applying the principles of concentration, mindfulness, and wisdom, one can use any experience as a stepping stone towards liberation.

### 9. All Phenomena Gain Their Footing in the Deathless State

In Buddhism, the "deathless state" has a profound dual meaning. On one hand, it refers to **Nibbāna**, the ultimate cessation of all phenomena and the end of the cycle of birth and death. On the other hand, the deathless state also signifies a condition where one is completely free from the fear of death. This freedom is attained by relinquishing the conceiving of self—the ego or identity that clings to existence and fears its cessation.

When all phenomena are correctly understood and transcended, they gain their footing in this deathless state. This means that by deeply comprehending the nature of phenomena and letting go of the notion of an enduring self, one can overcome the fear of death and enter the state of Nibbāna. In this state, there is no more birth, death, or suffering, and the mind is liberated from the cycles of existence.

The deathless state is, therefore, the culmination of all phenomena. It represents not only the end of the physical and mental formations that perpetuate existence but also the profound inner peace that comes from no longer fearing death. It is a state of ultimate freedom where one fully understands and experiences the true nature of reality, unburdened by the delusions of self and the anxieties of impermanence. 10. All Phenomena Have Nibbāna/Extinction as Their Final End

The final end of all phenomena is Nibbāna, also known as extinction or the stilling of all formations. Nibbāna is the ultimate goal of the Buddhist path, where all desires, attachments, and delusions are extinguished, and the mind is freed from the cycle of birth, death, and suffering.

Nibbāna is the cessation of all conditioned phenomena. It is the point at which all experiences, whether pleasurable or painful, come to an end. It represents the stilling of all activities and the ultimate liberation from the constraints of existence.

**Conclusion**

The Mulaka Sutta provides a profound understanding of the root of all phenomena, beginning with desire and culminating in Nibbāna. By tracing the sequence from desire to attention, contact, sensation, concentration, mindfulness, wisdom, liberation, and ultimately the deathless state, the sutta offers a comprehensive view of how experiences arise, are sustained, and can be transcended.

Through this understanding, one can begin to see how every experience, no matter how mundane or extraordinary, holds the potential for liberation. By applying concentration, mindfulness, and wisdom, one can use any experience as a gateway to the deathless state of Nibbāna, where all phenomena come to their final end in the stilling of all formations and the cessation of suffering.

# 9
# The First Step to Liberation: *Penetrative Attention (Yoniso Manasikāra)*

Penetrative attention, or Yoniso Manasikāra in Pali, is considered the first crucial step toward liberation in the teachings of Lord Buddha. To fully understand the significance of this practice, we must delve into the roots of the term itself. The word "yoni" translates to "vagina," symbolizing the starting point or the source of something. "Manasikāra" means "attention" or "mental engagement." Thus, Yoniso Manasikāra can be understood as directing our attention to the very origin, or the starting point, of all phenomena and experiences.

In our day-to-day lives, our attention is often focused outward. We perceive the world through our senses, interpreting what we see, hear, smell, taste, touch, and think as independent realities that exist outside of us. For instance, when we see an object, we assume that the visual experience exists independently of our cognition. When we hear a sound, we believe the sound exists on its own, apart from our perception of it. The same goes for other sensory experiences and even our thoughts; we think of them as reflections of actual, external problems or realities.

However, this outward focus is precisely what binds us to the cycle of suffering. Lord Buddha, in his infinite wisdom, invites us to shift our attention inward, toward the origin of these experiences. Instead of getting caught up in the external manifestations, we are encouraged to look within, to the very source from which these experiences arise.

To illustrate this, imagine a monkey in a room with six windows, constantly jumping from one window to another, trying to observe the outside world. This monkey is akin to our mind, which constantly shifts between different senses—sight, sound, smell, taste, touch, and thought—seeking satisfaction in the external world. Just as the monkey is never still, our minds are perpetually engaged in a series of cognitions, interpreting and reacting to what we perceive.

However, this process of cognition is not as straightforward as it seems. We often mistake the observed object and the observer—the self—as independent entities. But in reality, the notion of an "object" and a "self" only arises after the act of cognition. There is no "object" to be seen, nor a "self" to see it, until the mind has already processed the sensory data. The truth is that these experiences are not independent realities; they are mere fabrications of the mind, arising and passing away with each moment of cognition.

To further clarify this, imagine a dog crossing an old footbridge and noticing its shadow reflected in the water below. The dog, mistaking its shadow for another dog, starts barking at it or happily wagging its tail, thinking it has encountered a separate entity. The dog perceives the shadow as an independent being simply because it can see it, not realizing that the shadow is merely a reflection, not a separate dog.

Similarly, the experiences that arise from our six sense bases in this "robot-like" machine we call life are like the dog's shadow. We mistakenly perceive an independent world, believing that our experiences are rooted in external realities. In truth, this machine—our body and mind—can only recognize something when we pay attention to it. Just as the dog sees another dog due to its misperception, we perceive an independent world due to our own cognitive processes.

This misunderstanding highlights the need for **Yoniso Manasikāra**. By practicing Yoniso Manasikāra, we learn to pay attention to this internal mechanism rather than being swept away by the external stimuli. Instead of reacting to the content of our perceptions—whether pleasant, unpleasant, or neutral—we begin to observe the process itself. We become aware of the arising and passing away of cognitions one by one, without getting entangled in them.

For example, when a visual object comes into focus, instead of identifying it as "a tree" or "a car," we simply note the cognition of sight. When a sound arises, instead of labeling it as "music" or "noise," we recognize it as the cognition of hearing. This practice of seeing things as they truly are—as transient, conditioned phenomena—allows us to penetrate the superficial layers of perception and reach the core of our experiences.

This inward focus is akin to a robot examining its own programming. When a robot looks within its own mechanism rather than engaging with the data it processes, it sees the arising and passing of data as mere events. Similarly, when we apply Yoniso Manasikāra, we see our experiences as transient events, devoid of inherent meaning or substance.

Through this practice, we begin to understand the nature of reality more deeply. We see that all experiences, all phenomena, are merely passing events, not independent realities. This realization is the first step toward liberation. By understanding the impermanent and conditioned nature of our experiences, we can begin to detach from them, overcoming the cravings and aversions that lead to suffering.

In essence, Yoniso Manasikāra is not just a practice of paying attention; it is the practice of paying attention in the right way. It is the practice of penetrating beyond the surface of our experiences to see their true nature. By doing so, we lay the foundation for the path to liberation, as taught by Lord Buddha.

# 10
# The Heart of Buddhism:
## *Dependent Origination (Paṭicca Samuppāda)*

**Dependent Origination (Paṭicca Samuppāda)** is one of the most profound and essential teachings of Buddhism, often referred to as the "heart of Buddhism." It describes the chain of cause and effect that leads to the experience of suffering and the cycle of birth and death. Understanding this concept is crucial for those on the path to liberation.

### Two Approaches to Dependent Origination: Sutta Pitaka vs. Abhidhamma Pitaka

In the Buddhist scriptures, there are two primary ways that **Paṭicca Samuppāda** is presented: one in the **Sutta Pitaka** and the other in the **Abhidhamma Pitaka**. While both approaches aim to explain the same fundamental truth, they do so from slightly different perspectives, with the Sutta Pitaka's approach being more direct and practical, which Lord Buddha often emphasized.

1. **The Sutta Pitaka Approach**: The Sutta Pitaka emphasizes the immediacy of experience, focusing on how dependent origination unfolds in this very moment. It presents **Paṭicca Samuppāda** as a moment-to-moment process, where each link in the chain is dependent on the previous one, leading to the arising of suffering. This approach is practical and directly applicable to daily life and meditation, showing how ignorance and other mental factors arise and lead to suffering in the present moment.
2. **The Abhidhamma Pitaka Approach**: In contrast, the Abhidhamma Pitaka presents **Paṭicca Samuppāda** as a process that spans across three lifetimes—past, present, and future. It explains how actions (kamma) in a past life can give rise to experiences in the present life and how current actions will affect future rebirths. This approach delves deeply into the metaphysical aspects of existence, focusing on how karmic forces perpetuate the cycle of birth and death over time.

While the Abhidhamma's approach is valuable for understanding the broader scope of samsara (the cycle of birth, death, and rebirth), the Sutta Pitaka's method, which prioritizes the immediacy of cause and effect in the present moment, is often more accessible and directly applicable to practice. Therefore, we will prioritize the Sutta Pitaka's approach in this discussion.

**Understanding Dependent Origination (Paṭicca Samuppāda)**

**Paṭicca Samuppāda** is often explained through a twelve-link chain that begins with ignorance and ends with suffering. These links are interdependent, meaning that the presence of one leads to the arising of the next. The sequence is as follows:

**1. Avijjā (Ignorance):**

- **Definition:** Avijjā is the fundamental ignorance or lack of understanding regarding the true nature of reality, particularly the Four Noble Truths and the nature of anattā (non-self). It is the failure to see that all activities and preparations (physical, verbal, and mental) ultimately lead to stress and dissatisfaction.
- **Role:** Avijjā is the starting point of the chain. It obscures true understanding, causing beings to remain trapped in the cycle of samsāra (the cycle of birth, death, and rebirth).

**2. Saṅkhāra (Formations/Preparations):**

- **Definition:** Saṅkhāra refers to the physical, verbal, and mental preparations or activities. These range from basic bodily functions like breathing (breath in, breath out) to more complex physical actions. On the verbal level, they include everything from initial thoughts (vitakka: the initial application of the mind to an object) to sustained attention on that object (vicāra) and other verbal expressions. Mentally, saṅkhāra encompasses sensations, perceptions, and other mental formations conditioned by ignorance (avijjā). These formations include thoughts, actions, and intentions, all of which shape one's future experiences and existence.
- **Role:** Saṅkhāra plays a crucial role as the karmic formations that propel consciousness (viññāṇa) into new existences and experiences. Due to ignorance, beings create saṅkhāras, which in turn influence their actions. This ongoing cycle of creating and experiencing saṅkhāra leads to the arising of viññāṇa, the cognitions of the six sense bases: eye, ear, nose, tongue, body, and mind.

## 3. Viññāṇa (Consciousness/Cognition):

- **Definition:** Viññāṇa is the awareness or consciousness that arises as a result of saṅkhāras. It is the mind's capacity to recognize or be aware of something.

- **Role:** Viññāṇa is the link that connects the mental and physical components of existence. It is the initial spark of awareness that arises at conception and sets the stage for nāma-rūpa to develop.

## 4. Nāma-Rūpa (Name-and-Form):

- **Definition:** Nāma-rūpa refers to the combination of mental and physical components that constitute a being. The mental aspect (nāma) includes sensations, perceptions, intentions, contact, and attention, while the physical aspect (rūpa) encompasses the body and the elements that form the sense objects. These elements are primarily the four great elements: earth (patavi), water (apo), fire (tejo), and air (vayo), along with the various forms and structures derived from them.
- **Role:** Nāma-rūpa arises in dependence on viññāṇa (consciousness). This stage signifies the development of both mind and body, which are essential for experiencing the world. The interplay of nāma and rūpa provides the foundation for the six sense bases, allowing for the perception and interaction with the external world.

## 5. Saḷāyatana (Six Sense Bases):

- **Definition:** Saḷāyatana refers to the six sense bases: eye, ear, nose, tongue, body, and mind. These are the faculties through which beings perceive the world.
- **Role:** The six sense bases arise dependent on nāma-rūpa. With the development of the sense bases, beings are able to experience the world through sensory contact (phassa).

**6. Phassa (Contact):**

- **Definition:** Phassa is the contact or interaction between the sense bases, their corresponding objects, and consciousness. It is the moment when the sense organ, the sense object, and the corresponding consciousness come together.
- **Role:** Phassa arises dependent on the six sense bases. It leads to the arising of vedanā (feeling or sensation), which can be pleasant, unpleasant, or neutral. This contact is crucial as it lays the foundation for craving (taṇhā), which perpetuates the cycle of samsāra.

**7. Vedanā (Sensations):**

- **Definition:** Vedanā refers to the feelings or sensations that arise from contact (phassa) with the six sense bases. These feelings can be pleasant, unpleasant, or neutral/neither pleasant nor unpleasant.

- **Role:** Vedanā arises dependent on phassa. The experience of feeling is what often drives the next link in the chain: craving (taṇhā). For instance, when a pleasant feeling is experienced, there is a tendency to crave more of it, and when an unpleasant feeling is experienced, there is a tendency to resist or avoid it.

**8. Taṇhā (Craving):**

- **Definition:** Taṇhā is the craving or desire for sensory pleasures, existence, and non-existence. It is the strong urge to hold onto pleasurable experiences and avoid painful ones.
- **Role:** Taṇhā arises dependent on vedanā. Craving is a powerful force that perpetuates the cycle of samsāra, as beings continuously seek to satisfy their desires, leading to further suffering. Taṇhā is the root cause of suffering and is what keeps beings trapped in the cycle of rebirth.

**9. Upādāna (Clinging/Attachment):**

- **Definition:** Upādāna is the clinging or attachment that develops from craving. It involves holding onto objects, ideas, or desires with a strong sense of attachment.
- **Role:** Upādāna arises dependent on taṇhā. This attachment deepens the entanglement with samsāra, leading to further actions that reinforce

the cycle of suffering. It can manifest as attachment to sensual pleasures, views, rituals, or even the sense of self.

**10. Bhava (Existence):**

- **Definition:** Bhava refers to the process of becoming, particularly the sense or feeling of existence. It encompasses the perception that there is an independent world and that "I" exist within it. This feeling of existing lays the groundwork for future existence and rebirth, driven by the karmic activities shaped by craving and attachment.
- **Role:** Bhava arises dependent on upādāna (clinging). It is the stage where conditions are ripe for the manifestation of a new existence, preparing the way for birth into a specific realm within samsāra, whether it be human, animal, heavenly, or hellish.

**11. Jāti (Birth):**

- **Definition:** Jāti is the process of being born or the actual event of birth. It marks the beginning of a new existence within samsāra.
- **Role:** Jāti arises dependent on bhava. Once a being is born, the cycle of samsāra continues, bringing with it the inevitable experiences of aging, death, and other forms of suffering.

**12. Jarā-Maraṇa (Aging and Death):**

- **Definition:** Jarā refers to aging, and maraṇa refers to death. Together, they encompass the full range of suffering experienced in life, including sorrow, lamentation, pain, grief, and despair.
- **Role:** Jarā-maraṇa arises dependent on jāti. This final link in the chain represents the culmination of the cycle of suffering, as every being who is born must experience aging, decay, and eventually death. The cycle then continues unless the chain of dependent origination is broken.

**Summary of the Full Chain of Dependent Origination:**

1. **Avijjā** (Ignorance) → conditions the arising of **Saṅkhāra** (Preparations)
2. **Saṅkhāra** (Preparations) → conditions the arising of **Viññāṇa** (Consciousness)
3. **Viññāṇa** (Consciousness) → conditions the arising of **Nāma-Rūpa** (Name-and-Form)
4. **Nāma-Rūpa** (Name-and-Form) → conditions the arising of **Saḷāyatana** (Six Sense Bases)
5. **Saḷāyatana** (Six Sense Bases) → conditions the arising of **Phassa** (Contact)
6. **Phassa** (Contact) → conditions the arising of **Vedanā** (Feeling)
7. **Vedanā** (Feeling) → conditions the arising of **Taṇhā** (Craving)
8. **Taṇhā** (Craving) → conditions the arising of **Upādāna** (Clinging)

9. **Upādāna** (Clinging) → conditions the arising of **Bhava** (Existence/Becoming)
10. **Bhava** (Existence/Becoming) → conditions the arising of **Jāti** (Birth)
11. **Jāti** (Birth) → conditions the arising of **Jarā-Maraṇa** (Aging and Death)

**The Cycle of Craving: A Luxury Car Obsession**

Imagine a man who is deeply obsessed with luxury cars, particularly the Rolls-Royce Phantom or the Mercedes-Benz Maybach S-Class. Every time he sees one of these cars, his mind is instantly captivated. This obsession stems from ignorance—his inability to recognize that the activities he engages in, driven by his desire for these cars, are ultimately stressful and unsatisfactory.

Due to this ignorance, he begins to engage in various preparations, both physical and mental. He might try to touch or drive the car, eagerly engage in conversations about it with the owner, or spend countless hours fantasizing and planning how he might one day acquire such a vehicle.

This entire process is rooted in ignorance (not recognizing the inherent stress in these activities), which gives rise to preparations (the desire and efforts to experience the car). These preparations condition his consciousness (his awareness and thoughts about the car). This consciousness, in turn, interacts with name-and-form (the mental and physical components of his being), resulting in the activation of the six sense bases (such as sight and touch), leading to contact (the experience of seeing or touching the car).

From this contact arises a feeling (the pleasure derived from experiencing the car), which naturally leads to craving (a deep-seated desire to own or experience the car again). This craving then leads to clinging (an attachment to the idea of possessing the car, where the car becomes his entire world). These clinging conditions his sense of existence (the desire to continue being someone who owns or enjoys luxury cars, reinforcing the illusion of an independent self and world).

Finally, this sense of existence, rooted in his attachment to the car, sets the stage for rebirth. This rebirth then subjects him to aging and death—the inevitable decline in satisfaction as circumstances change—ultimately resulting in sorrow, grief, and a profound sense of loss. In this way, the man becomes trapped in the cycle of dependent origination, where each step fuels the next, perpetuating his suffering.

**The Cycle of Consciousness and Name-Form**

In the intricate framework of **Paṭicca Samuppāda** (Dependent Origination), one of the most profound aspects is the interdependent relationship between **consciousness (Viññāṇa)** and **name-form (Nāma-Rūpa)**. These two elements are deeply intertwined, sustaining and reinforcing each other in a cyclical process that perpetuates the cycle of existence.

Consciousness provides the foundation for the arising of name-form, which encompasses both mental activities (such as sensations, perceptions, intentions, contact, and attention) and physical components (such as the body and sense objects). In other words, because of consciousness, these mental and material phenomena come into being within an individual's inner world.

Conversely, name-form provides the necessary conditions for consciousness to continue. The physical body and the mental processes it supports—like the brain's functions—allow consciousness to manifest through various cognitions. This mutual dependence creates a feedback loop: consciousness sustains name-form, and name-form, in turn, sustains consciousness.

**Example:**

To illustrate this concept, imagine a person who is deeply engaged in the experience of a beautiful landscape.

When they first see the landscape, **consciousness** arises in relation to the visual form. This consciousness allows the landscape to be perceived, giving rise to the **name-form**—the mental image and physical sensation of seeing the landscape. The mind recognizes the beauty, categorizes the experience through sensations and perceptions, and forms intentions and emotions related to the scene.

Because of this **name-form**, the person's consciousness continues to interact with the landscape. Their mind becomes absorbed in the beauty, generating thoughts, emotions, and further perceptions, which, in turn, reinforce the initial consciousness. This process perpetuates a cycle where the consciousness of the landscape and the mental and physical phenomena associated with it continue to sustain each other.

In essence, the person's experience of the landscape is a result of the **mutual dependence** between consciousness and name-form. This interdependence keeps the cycle of existence turning, trapping the individual in a loop of continued experience and attachment.

By understanding this cycle, one can begin to see how deeply rooted consciousness and name-form are in sustaining the illusion of an independent and enduring self. Breaking free from this cycle is essential for liberation, as it involves seeing through the interdependence and impermanence of these phenomena.

**Conclusion:**

The flow of dependent origination describes the process by which ignorance leads to a chain of causally linked events, culminating in birth, aging, and death, perpetuating the cycle of suffering (dukkha). By understanding and breaking this chain—particularly through the cessation of craving (taṇhā) and ignorance (avijjā)—one can achieve liberation (nibbāna) and escape the cycle of samsāra.

# 11
# What is Liberation?
## *The Cessation of Suffering*

Liberation, or Nibbāna, is the ultimate goal in Buddhist practice—the complete cessation of suffering. The Pali phrase that captures the essence of Nibbāna is: "**Etaṃ santaṃ, etaṃ paṇītaṃ, yadidaṃ sabba-saṅkhāra-samatho, sabbūpadhipaṭinissaggo, taṇhākkhayo, virāgo, nirodho, nibbānaṃ.**" which translates to: "This is peaceful, this is excellent, namely, the stilling of all preparations, the relinquishment of assets, the destruction of craving, dispassion/detachment, cessation, extinction." At its core, Nibbāna is the stilling of all physical, verbal and mental preparations (sankhāras). It is not a distant goal to be achieved in the future or in another life; liberation can be attained here and now by extinguishing ignorance.

Once this state is reached, one is entirely free from the illusion of self and liberated from all forms of suffering and stress. The liberated person transcends the cycle of existence—*saṃsāra*—by living fully in the present moment, with intense awareness. By not identifying with the concept of self, the liberated one will not be reborn, as there is no longer any fuel—clinging—that leads to the formation of a new existence. Liberation is a profound mental state characterized by the stilling of all preparations: the stilling of breath, stilling of pre-verbal engagements like initial application and sustained attention, and stilling of all sensations and perceptions.

When one experiences the full level of liberation by absorbing into it, even the perception of liberation itself fades away. In this profound state, the sense of self or existence no longer persists; there is no "I" to perceive or experience liberation. The observer dissolves entirely, revealing that the observer was merely another form of observation. As a result, one cannot even enjoy the pleasant sensations of enlightenment, because we can only enjoy what we can perceive. It's as if, through deep understanding, one turns off the very mechanism of existence.

To illustrate, let's revisit the example of the luxury car enthusiast. When he fully comprehends that all forms of physical, verbal, and mental preparations are inherently stressful, wisdom arises, and ignorance dissipates. With this insight, he can "turn off" his craving and clinging, leading to a cessation of the cycle of suffering.

A person who attains liberation can sit quietly, close their eyes, and still all preparations—breathing, thinking, perceiving—sensing thus disconnecting from all forms of existence. In this state, there is no consciousness of the world or self; no engagement with name-form, no activation of the six sense bases, no contact, no sensation, no craving, no clinging, no becoming, and consequently, no birth. The end of birth signifies the end of decay, death, and suffering. An enlightened person, therefore, is not only free from future birth, decay, and death but is also free from these in the current life, as they have transcended the idea of self and existence.

The most profound insight from the teaching of Paṭicca Samuppāda (Dependent Origination) is that by breaking the chain—particularly at the link of ignorance—one can bring the entire cycle of suffering to an end. When ignorance is replaced by wisdom, the subsequent links in the chain no longer arise, leading to the cessation of suffering.

For example, if our car enthusiast gains insight into the true nature of his obsession, he may come to realize that the pleasure derived from the car is fleeting and ultimately leads to stress. With this understanding, he can stop engaging in the mental and physical activities that fuel his craving and attachment, thereby breaking the cycle of dependent origination. Rather than continuing to make preparations, he can allow all preparations to cease by entering the state of enlightenment, where even breathing, thinking, perceiving, and sensing are stilled.

In this way, by cultivating wisdom and insight into the true nature of phenomena, one can attain liberation from the cycle of birth, death, and suffering.

# 12
# The Four Stages of Liberation:
## *From Stream-Entry to Full Enlightenment*

When a person experiences the stilling of all preparations (*sankhāra*) for the very first time, even if only for a few seconds, they reach the stage known as "Sotāpanna" or "stream-enterer." This is the first step on the path to liberation, where the individual has entered the stream that inevitably leads to Nibbāna. A Sotāpanna is assured of reaching complete liberation within a maximum of seven more lives and will never again be reborn in the animal realm or any other hellish worlds. Once this stage is achieved, nothing can prevent the person from attaining full liberation.

Liberation unfolds in four stages:

1. **Stream-Entry (Sotāpanna)**: Upon experiencing the stilling of all preparations for the first time, the

Sotāpanna automatically begins to "turn off" from the cycle of physical, verbal, and mental activities that lead to suffering. They become deeply aware of the stressfulness inherent in these preparations and develop a natural inclination to detach from them. This marks the beginning of the path to liberation.

2. **Once-Returner (Sakadāgāmi)**: As the Sotāpanna continues to practice, their attachment to lust, greed, and aversion diminishes by 50%. When this occurs, they reach the second stage, known as Sakadāgāmi, or "once-returner." A Sakadāgāmi is destined to be reborn only once more in the human realm or in a heavenly realm before attaining full enlightenment.
3. **Non-Returner (Anāgāmi)**: By deepening their practice and wisdom, the Sakadāgāmi eventually eradicates lust, greed, and aversion completely, reaching the third stage of liberation known as Anāgāmi, or "non-returner." An Anāgāmi will not be reborn in the human realm or in any of the heavenly realms but may be reborn in a *Brahma* realm, where beings subsist on meditative ecstasy. In this stage, if full enlightenment is not attained in the current life, it will be pursued in the next.
4. **Arahant (Fully Enlightened)**: The final stage of liberation is becoming an Arahant, a fully enlightened being who has completely turned off from the cycle of existence. For an Anāgāmi to reach this stage, they must overcome the most subtle and acute clinging to the concept of self. According to

> Lord Buddha, if one practices the path of liberation with diligence and heedfulness, complete enlightenment can be attained within a period ranging from seven days to seven years. If achieving full enlightenment within this timeframe proves challenging, reaching the Anāgāmi stage is still assured within seven years.

The Dhamma, the teaching of liberation, is timeless. This path is realistic and achievable even in contemporary times, as modern psychology supports the idea that consistent practice rewires the brain within a period of around seven years.

Once someone attains full enlightenment, they view death not as a threat but as a natural culmination of their journey, much like an employee awaiting their salary. When death arrives, an enlightened person already relinquished his life without any clinging, ensuring that they will not be reborn in any realm. They have transcended the cycle of birth, death, and suffering, and have achieved the ultimate peace and freedom that is Nibbāna.

# 13
# The Fearfulness of Saṃsāra: *Understanding the Cycle of Birth and Death*

Saṃsāra, in Buddhist teachings, refers to the endless cycle of birth, death, and rebirth that all beings are trapped in until they attain enlightenment. It is a cycle driven by ignorance, craving, and karma, leading to continuous suffering. While some may dismiss the concept of saṃsāra as a mere fairytale, a closer examination of life's inherent suffering and the stark inequalities we observe around us reveals its profound truth.

**The Nature of Saṃsāra**

Saṃsāra is characterized by constant change, instability, and suffering. Every being, regardless of their status, is subject to aging, illness, death, and the sorrow that comes with attachment and loss. This endless cycle is perpetuated by our ignorance of the true nature of reality and our clinging to the idea of a permanent self.

In this cycle, our actions (karma) have profound consequences. Every thought, word, and deed create ripples that affect not just this life but future lives as well. Good deeds may lead to favorable rebirths, while negative actions can result in suffering in future lives. This is why some are born into wealth and beauty, while others are born into poverty and suffering. These disparities are not the result of a capricious or unjust god, but rather the natural outcome of the karmic seeds planted in past lives.

**The Fearfulness of Saṃsāra**

Saṃsāra is inherently fearful because it offers no true refuge or lasting happiness. Even the most fortunate lives are marred by suffering, whether it be through the inevitable decline of the body, the loss of loved ones, or the anxiety that comes with change. The relentless nature of saṃsāra means that as long as we are caught in this cycle, we will continue to experience suffering, with no end in sight.

Consider the inequalities in the world: some are born into privilege, while others suffer from birth. This is not random; it is the result of past karma. The idea that our current life circumstances are shaped by past actions emphasizes the seriousness of our situation. If we continue to act out of ignorance and craving, we will only perpetuate our suffering, lifetime after lifetime.

The Buddha illustrated the horror of saṃsāra with powerful examples. He taught that the amount of blood shed from being slaughtered as a cow in our countless past lives is more than the water in all the oceans. The tears we have shed in saṃsāra, particularly when separated from loved ones, exceed the water in the entire ocean. He also explained that saṃsāra is not confined to this Earth alone. The universe contains billions of other Earths, each with its own realms and beings. In every solar system, there are 31 realms of existence, ranging from the hells, animal worlds, and hungry ghost realms to the human world, various heavens, and the Brahma worlds. When one Earth perishes, the cycle continues on another, trapping us indefinitely in this cosmic cycle of suffering.

**Why We Must Seek Liberation**

Given the inherent suffering in saṃsāra, the only true solution is to seek liberation through enlightenment. Enlightenment, or Nibbāna, is the cessation of all suffering and the end of the cycle of rebirth. It is the state of ultimate peace, where ignorance, craving, and the false notion of self are extinguished.

To reach enlightenment, one must cultivate wisdom and understanding, breaking free from the chains of karma and delusion. This path requires a deep commitment to ethical conduct, mental discipline, and the development of insight. The journey is challenging, but the alternative is to remain trapped in the endless cycle of suffering.

Saṃsāra is not a fairytale; it is the reality of our existence. The social differences we observe, the inequalities and injustices, all point to the underlying truth of karma and rebirth. By understanding the true nature of saṃsāra and contemplating the Buddha's teachings on the enormity of our suffering through countless lifetimes, we can cultivate a sense of urgency to break free from this cycle and attain the ultimate peace of enlightenment.

# 14
# The Best Answer to Most of Our Problems:
## *A Deep Dive into Reflections on Repulsiveness (Patikkula Manasikāra)*

Life is filled with challenges and sufferings that often seem inescapable. We crave love and validation, struggle with feelings of inferiority, envy the luxuries others possess, and constantly strive to achieve dreams that seem to promise happiness. But why do we suffer so much? Why do these desires and disappointments weigh so heavily on us? The root cause lies in our profound ignorance of the true nature of the body—our own and that of others. We are enamored by the surface, the appearance, while utterly unaware of the repulsive reality that lies beneath.

From the moment we are born, we are conditioned to view the body as something desirable and beautiful. Society reinforces this illusion through media, culture, and even personal relationships. We invest so much energy into maintaining this appearance—grooming, dressing up, and adorning ourselves—all in the hope of gaining love, admiration, and respect. But what are we truly admiring? What are we clinging to? Beneath the surface, every body is filled with elements that are fundamentally repulsive.

**The Reality of the Human Body**

Consider the basic functions of the human body. Every day, we must expel waste through urination and defecation, we sweat, our bodies produce mucus, pus, and other fluids that are anything but unpleasant. Even the most attractive individuals are not exempt from these processes. The beautiful girl admired by many, or the handsome man envied by all, still must visit the bathroom multiple times a day. Their feces smell just as foul, their sweat can stink, and their bodies can produce the same unpleasant fluids as anyone else's. Yet, we conveniently ignore these facts, focusing only on the outer appearance.

Let's take a more vivid example. Imagine the most beautiful person in the world—someone who is the epitome of physical attractiveness. Now, imagine this person being confined in a room, unable to leave for several days. In just three to four days, the reality of their physical existence would become painfully obvious. The room would fill with the stench of their unwashed body, the smell of their feces and urine, and the rancid odor of their sweat. The very presence of this person, who was once considered beautiful, would become unbearable. The illusion of beauty would be shattered, replaced by the undeniable reality of the body's repulsiveness.

And what about death? The most handsome or beautiful person, after death, quickly becomes a repulsive sight. Within days, the body begins to swell, turns blue, and starts to decay. The flesh decomposes, the stench becomes overpowering, and the body is soon eaten by worms, insects, and scavenging animals. The once-admired body, now lifeless, is reduced to a decaying corpse, eventually becoming nothing more than a skeleton.

**The Present Moment of Repulsiveness**

But the repulsiveness of the body is not just something that manifests in death; it is ever-present, even in life. Every single human being, no matter how clean or attractive they may seem, carries around at least 50 grams of feces inside their intestines. Our bodies are essentially machines made up of bones, muscles, blood, and various organs that are, by their very nature, repulsive. The skin that covers this machine is only a thin layer, beneath which lies a complex network of nerves, blood vessels, and tissues.

Take, for example, the simple act of kissing someone on the forehead. What are we really doing? We are pressing our lips against a thin layer of skin, beneath which is a thin layer of flesh, and under that lies the skull. In essence, when we kiss someone, we are kissing a skeleton covered by a thin veneer of flesh. Yet, we romanticize this act, completely ignoring the true nature of the body we are so affectionately embracing.

**The Practice of Patikkula Manasikāra in Buddhism**

In Buddhism, the practice of Patikkula Manasikāra, or reflections on repulsiveness, is a powerful meditation technique that helps us to see the body as it truly is. Lord Buddha encouraged his disciples to meditate on the body by dividing it into its 32 parts, including skin, flesh, bones, blood, organs, and fluids. By deeply contemplating each of these components, we begin to realize that there is no inherent beauty or desirability in the body—only a collection of impermanent, repulsive elements.

This practice is not meant to create a sense of disgust or self-loathing but rather to cultivate a deep understanding of the true nature of the body. When we see the body for what it truly is, we can begin to detach ourselves from the illusions that cause so much of our suffering. We no longer feel the need to impress others or seek validation through physical appearance. The desire for social status, luxury, or admiration loses its grip on us because we realize that the body, we are trying to glorify is nothing more than a temporary vessel filled with repulsive elements.

**The Liberation from Attachment**

When we truly understand the repulsiveness of the body, a profound transformation occurs. We no longer cling to the illusion of beauty, nor do we become attached to the bodies of others. This detachment leads to a liberation from many of the problems that plague us—problems rooted in desire, attachment, and the need for validation.

For example, consider the desire to be loved by someone. This desire often leads to feelings of inferiority, jealousy, and even despair when that love is not reciprocated. But when we see the true nature of the body, we realize that the object of our desire is nothing more than a collection of repulsive elements, just like ourselves. The illusion of romantic love fades, replaced by a deeper understanding of the impermanence and unsatisfactory nature of physical existence.

Similarly, the pursuit of luxury and status, often driven by a desire to impress others, becomes meaningless when we understand the repulsiveness of the body. Why should we care about the approval of others when the very bodies we are trying to impress are themselves impermanent and filled with repulsive elements? This realization frees us from the endless cycle of desire and dissatisfaction, allowing us to find true contentment in the reality of existence.

**The Path to Liberation**

The understanding of the repulsiveness of the body and the fearfulness of saṃsāra are powerful motivators for seeking liberation. By reflecting on the true nature of the body and the endless cycle of suffering, we can develop a strong sense of renunciation, a desire to break free from the cycle of birth and death.

Liberation, in Buddhist terms, is not about escaping life, but rather about transcending the illusion of self and the attachment to physical existence. When we realize that the body is just a temporary vessel filled with repulsive elements, we can begin to detach from the desires and attachments that bind us to saṃsāra. This detachment leads to the cultivation of wisdom, which is the key to breaking free from the cycle of suffering.

By practicing mindfulness, meditation, and the reflection on repulsiveness, we can gradually weaken our attachment to the body and the illusions that cause suffering. This practice leads to the development of insight into the true nature of reality, ultimately culminating in the attainment of enlightenment—Nibbāna.

Nibbāna is the state of ultimate liberation, where the cycle of birth and death is finally broken. It is the cessation of all suffering, the end of Saṃsāra.

# 15
# Acceptance is the Key to Happiness

Happiness is often seen as something to be pursued, a goal to be achieved by acquiring certain things or reaching specific milestones in life. However, true happiness is not found in external achievements or material possessions but in the way we perceive and respond to life as it unfolds. One of the most profound teachings in Buddhism, and indeed in many spiritual traditions, is that "Acceptance is the key to happiness." This concept is rooted in understanding the nature of existence, the impermanence of all things, and the importance of living in the present moment.

**The Illusion of Past and Future**

Much of our suffering arises from our attachment to the past and our anxiety about the future. We dwell on past mistakes, lost opportunities, and moments of pain, allowing these memories to haunt our present. Conversely, we often live in anticipation of the future, worrying about what might happen, chasing after dreams, and fearing the unknown. Both of these tendencies distract us from the present moment, the only time that truly exists.

In Buddhism, it is taught that the past and future are merely thoughts, constructs of the mind that have no real substance. The past is gone, and the future is yet to come; the only reality we have is the present moment. By accepting this, we can free ourselves from the burden of regret and the anxiety of anticipation. Acceptance means letting go of the past and not clinging to the future, allowing us to fully experience and appreciate the present.

**The Power of Being Present**

When we accept the present moment as it is, without judgment or resistance, we open ourselves to a deeper level of contentment and peace. This does not mean passively enduring whatever comes our way but rather embracing each experience with mindfulness and gratitude. Being present means being fully engaged with whatever we are doing, whether it is a mundane task or a moment of joy. It is about finding beauty and meaning in the here and now, rather than in some imagined future or idealized past.

Be grateful for this moment, every moment is a gift, an opportunity to grow, learn, and experience life. Even in difficult times, acceptance allows us to see the lessons and growth potential in our challenges. Instead of resisting or wishing things were different, we learn to flow with life, adapting to whatever comes our way.

**Enjoying the Present Intensely**

One of the most powerful ways to cultivate happiness through acceptance is to enjoy the present moment intensely. This means engaging with life without the interference of imaginations and conceivings. When we let go of preconceived notions, expectations, and fantasies, we can fully immerse ourselves in the present experience. Whether we are spending time with loved ones, working on a project, or simply enjoying a quiet moment alone, the key is to be fully present, savouring the moment without distraction.

In Buddhist practice, this is often cultivated through mindfulness, a state of awareness where we observe our thoughts, feelings, and sensations without attachment or aversion. By practicing mindfulness, we learn to accept our experiences as they are, without labelling them as good or bad. This non-judgmental awareness allows us to experience life more fully and deeply, leading to a profound sense of peace and contentment.

**Acceptance of Every Moment and Experience**

Acceptance also means embracing every moment and every experience, no matter how pleasant or unpleasant it may be. Life is a constant flow of change, with highs and lows, joys and sorrows. By accepting this impermanence, we learn to ride the waves of life without being overwhelmed by them. We understand that everything is temporary, and this understanding helps us not to cling to the good times or resist the bad times.

In Buddhism, this concept is closely related to the teaching of "non-self" or "anatta." The idea is that there is no permanent, unchanging self; instead, we are a collection of experiences, thoughts, and sensations that are constantly in flux. By accepting this, we realize that our suffering often comes from our attachment to an illusory self and the desire for things to be different from what they are. Acceptance allows us to let go of this attachment and find peace in the present moment, just as it is.

**Practical Ways to Cultivate Acceptance**

To cultivate acceptance, start by practicing mindfulness in your daily life. Pay attention to your thoughts and feelings without judgment, and gently bring your focus back to the present moment whenever you find yourself drifting into the past or future. Develop gratitude for the small, everyday experiences that make up your life, and learn to appreciate the beauty in the ordinary.

Another powerful practice is to reflect on the impermanence of all things. Remind yourself that everything is temporary, including your thoughts, emotions, and experiences. This can help you to accept whatever comes your way, knowing that it will pass.

Finally, embrace the Buddhist practice of "Patikkula Manasikara" or reflections on repulsiveness. This involves contemplating the repulsive aspects of the body and material existence to reduce attachment and desire. By realizing that even the most beautiful or desirable things in life have their unpleasant aspects, you can develop a more balanced and accepting view of life.

**Conclusion**

In conclusion, acceptance is indeed the key to happiness. By letting go of our attachment to the past and future, embracing the present moment, and accepting life as it is, we can find true peace and contentment. This is not a passive resignation to fate but an active engagement with life in a way that is mindful, grateful, and free from the illusion of self. Through acceptance, we can break free from the cycle of suffering and find lasting happiness in the here and now.

# 16
# The Lord Buddha:
## *The Fully Self-Enlightened One*

### The Luxurious Life of Prince Siddhartha

Before He became known as the Lord Buddha, Siddhartha Gautama was a prince, born into the royal family of the Shakya clan in ancient India. His early life was marked by luxury, comfort, and opulence. As the only son of King Suddhodana and Queen Maya, Siddhartha was groomed to inherit the throne and lead a life of power and privilege. The king, wishing to shield his son from the harsh realities of the world, provided him with every conceivable luxury. Siddhartha lived in a series of palaces, each one more magnificent than the last, designed to cater to every season of the year. He was surrounded by attendants, musicians, dancers, and servants who were devoted to ensuring his happiness.

Siddhartha was married to the beautiful Princess Yasodhara, and together they had a son, Rahula. His life seemed perfect: he had a loving family, wealth, and all the pleasures that life could offer. He was an accomplished athlete, skilled in archery, horse riding, and swordsmanship. His days were filled with entertainment, from watching dances and theatrical performances to engaging in sports and enjoying the finest foods.

However, despite all the luxuries and pleasures at his disposal, Siddhartha began to sense that something was missing. He noticed that the joy he derived from these pleasures was fleeting and that no matter how much he indulged, a deep sense of dissatisfaction remained. He realized that the happiness provided by worldly pleasures was temporary, and with each passing day, this realization grew stronger.

**The Search for True Liberation**

Siddhartha's realization that material pleasures could not provide lasting happiness led him to question the very nature of existence. He began to notice the inherent unsatisfactoriness (dukkha) of life. The impermanence of joy, the inevitability of decay, and the certainty of death weighed heavily on his mind. Even the most pleasurable experiences eventually became monotonous and unsatisfying. He understood that no matter how many luxuries he enjoyed, they could never bring an end to his inner restlessness.

This growing awareness prompted Siddhartha to seek something beyond the transient pleasures of the world. He realized that the cycle of craving and clinging was the source of his dissatisfaction. The more he indulged in worldly pleasures, the more he found himself trapped in a never-ending cycle of desire and disappointment. He saw that true happiness could not be found in external things but had to be discovered within.

One day, Siddhartha encountered the famous "Four Sights" that would change the course of his life forever. During a visit outside the palace, he saw an old man, a sick person, a corpse, and a wandering ascetic. These sights made him realize the inevitability of aging, sickness, and death, and they deepened his resolve to find a solution to the problem of suffering. He understood that true liberation could only be achieved by transcending the cycle of birth, decay, and death.

**The Renunciation and Spiritual Quest**

Driven by his desire to find the ultimate truth, Siddhartha made the bold decision to renounce his princely life. At the age of 29, he left the palace, his family, and all his worldly possessions in search of the path to enlightenment. He became a wandering ascetic, practicing severe austerities and meditation in the hope of discovering the truth about existence and the way to end suffering.

For six years, Siddhartha practiced extreme forms of self-mortification, pushing his body to its limits in an attempt to conquer his desires and achieve liberation. However, he eventually realized that neither indulgence in luxury nor self-denial could lead to enlightenment. This insight led him to discover the Middle Way—a path of moderation that avoids the extremes of both sensual indulgence and self-torture.

**The Enlightenment of the Lord Buddha**

At the age of 35, Siddhartha sat under the Bodhi tree in Bodh Gaya, vowing not to rise until he had attained enlightenment. After a night of deep meditation, he finally achieved his goal. He experienced the ultimate realization of the nature of reality, the cessation of suffering, and the end of the cycle of birth and death. In that moment, Siddhartha became the Lord Buddha, the Fully Self-Enlightened One.

The Lord Buddha's enlightenment was not just an intellectual understanding but a profound inner transformation. He saw the true nature of existence: that all phenomena are impermanent, that craving leads to suffering, and that by eliminating craving, one can attain liberation from the cycle of samsara. He understood that the self is an illusion and that clinging to the idea of a permanent self is the root cause of suffering. With this understanding, He achieved Nibbana, a state of complete freedom from suffering, desire, and ignorance.

## The Lord Buddha as a Holy and Enlightened Being

The Lord Buddha's enlightenment transformed Him into a being of unparalleled wisdom, compassion, and holiness. He spent the rest of His life teaching the Dhamma—the truth He had discovered—to all who were willing to listen. His teachings were not based on dogma or blind faith but on His direct experience of reality. He taught that every individual has the potential to achieve enlightenment by following the Noble Eightfold Path, a path of ethical conduct, mental discipline, and wisdom.

The Lord Buddha's holiness was not just in His wisdom but in His boundless compassion for all beings. He dedicated His life to helping others free themselves from the bonds of ignorance and suffering. His teachings were universal, applicable to all people regardless of their background, and they continue to inspire millions to this day.

## The Holiness of the Sangha

The Lord Buddha's disciples, the Sangha, were those who followed His teachings and dedicated themselves to the path of enlightenment. The Sangha became a community of holy beings, individuals who, through their practice, had overcome the illusions of self and attachment. The monks and nuns of the Sangha lived lives of simplicity, renunciation, and meditation, striving to purify their minds and attain the same enlightenment that the Lord Buddha had realized.

Many of the Lord Buddha's disciples became Arahants, fully enlightened beings who had eradicated all defilements and attained Nibbana. These disciples were revered as saints, having transcended the ordinary human condition and achieved a state of perfect peace and wisdom. The holiness of the Sangha lies in their commitment to the Dhamma and their realization of the ultimate truth, making them beings of profound spiritual stature, higher than ordinary beings who are still trapped in the cycle of samsara.

**Conclusion**

The story of the Lord Buddha is one of profound transformation—from a life of luxury and privilege to the attainment of ultimate liberation. The Lord Buddha's journey serves as an inspiration to all who seek true happiness and freedom from suffering. His realization of the unsatisfactory nature of worldly pleasures led Him to renounce everything and seek the ultimate truth. Through His enlightenment, He discovered the path to the cessation of suffering, a path that He shared with the world out of compassion for all beings.

The Lord Buddha's holiness, wisdom, and compassion continue to shine as a beacon of hope and guidance for those who seek liberation. His disciples, the Sangha, carry forward His teachings, embodying the same holiness and wisdom that the Lord Buddha exemplified. Together, they offer a path to transcend the illusions of life and attain the highest spiritual realization, inspiring countless individuals to follow in their footsteps and seek the ultimate liberation that the Lord Buddha discovered.

# 17
# The Importance of Refuge and Precepts on the Path to Liberation

**Understanding the True Refuge**

On the journey to attain liberation, it is crucial to recognize that there is no refuge in this universe other than the Triple Gem: the Lord Buddha, the Dhamma, and the Sangha. These three represent the ultimate source of guidance, support, and
protection on the path to Nibbana, the cessation of all suffering.

1. **The Lord Buddha**: The Lord Buddha is the fully self-enlightened one who discovered the path to liberation through His own efforts and wisdom. He is the one who shows us the way out of suffering, having walked the path Himself. His life and teachings are a testament to the possibility of attaining complete freedom from the cycle of birth

and death. The Lord Buddha's compassion and wisdom are boundless, and by taking refuge in Him, we align ourselves with His example and guidance.

2. **The Dhamma**: The Dhamma represents the teachings and methods that the Lord Buddha expounded to help us overcome suffering. It is the truth of existence—the reality of impermanence, suffering, and non-self. The Dhamma provides the practical steps that we must take to purify our minds, develop wisdom, and attain Nibbana. It is the path that leads us to the cessation of suffering, the ultimate goal of every being. Taking refuge in the Dhamma means committing ourselves to study, understand, and practice these teachings in our daily lives.
3. **The Sangha**: The Sangha consists of the Lord Buddha's disciples who have dedicated their lives to practicing the path He taught. They are the ones who have realized, or are on the way to realizing, the truth of the Dhamma and have become role models for those who seek liberation. The Sangha serves as a guide and a source of inspiration, showing us that it is possible to attain the same liberation that the Lord Buddha achieved. By taking refuge in the Sangha, we trust in their wisdom, guidance, and support on our spiritual journey.

When we truly understand and take refuge in the Lord Buddha, the Dhamma, and the Sangha, we recognize that there is no other refuge in this world that can lead us to liberation. Everything else—whether it be wealth, power, relationships, or material comforts—is impermanent and ultimately unsatisfactory. Only the Triple Gem offers a refuge that leads to the end of suffering.

**The Role of Faith in the Path to Liberation**

Faith, or *saddha*, is a vital component of the spiritual path. It is the trust and confidence we place in the Triple Gem as our true refuge. Without faith, our commitment to the path wavers, and we are susceptible to distractions and deviations. The journey to liberation is not easy, and without strong faith, we might abandon the path when faced with difficulties or temptations.

For example, consider a person who begins practicing meditation with enthusiasm but lacks deep faith in the Triple Gem. Over time, they may encounter challenges such as restlessness, doubt, or the allure of worldly pleasures. Without faith, they may give up, believing that the path is too difficult or that other pursuits might offer quicker or more tangible rewards. In contrast, a person with strong faith remains steadfast, trusting that the path of the Lord Buddha is the only way to true and lasting happiness.

Faith energizes us, giving us the motivation to persist in our practice even when we face obstacles. It provides the foundation for our efforts, ensuring that we continue to progress toward liberation, no matter how challenging the journey may be.

**The Five Precepts: A Foundation for Liberation**

To progress on the path to liberation, it is essential to establish a solid foundation of ethical conduct. The Lord Buddha taught the Five Precepts as basic guidelines for moral behaviour, which serve as the groundwork for mental purification and spiritual development. These precepts are:

1. **Refrain from Killing Beings**: All living beings value their lives and fear death. By refraining from killing, we cultivate compassion and respect for life. For example, even the smallest insect struggles to survive, and by choosing not to harm it, we practice non-violence and kindness. This precept helps us develop a mind that is free from cruelty and aggression, qualities that hinder spiritual progress.
2. **Refrain from Stealing**: Taking what is not freely given creates feelings of guilt, fear, and dishonesty, which disturb our peace of mind. By refraining from stealing, we cultivate honesty and contentment with what we have. For instance, a person who abstains from taking another's property, even when no one is watching, strengthens their integrity and builds trustworthiness. This precept helps us develop a mind that is free from greed and deceit.
3. **Refrain from Sexual Misconduct**: Sexual misconduct, such as infidelity or exploiting others for sexual pleasure, causes harm and suffering to ourselves and others. It disrupts relationships and leads to feelings of shame, guilt, and turmoil. By

refraining from sexual misconduct, we cultivate respect and responsibility in our relationships. For example, remaining faithful to one's partner nurtures trust and harmony in the relationship, contributing to inner peace and stability. This precept helps us develop a mind that is free from lust and harmful desires.

4. **Refrain from Lying**: Truthfulness is essential for maintaining trust and harmony in society. Lying creates confusion, mistrust, and a lack of integrity. By refraining from lying, we cultivate honesty and clarity in our communication. For instance, speaking the truth, even when it is difficult, fosters mutual respect and understanding. This precept helps us develop a mind that is free from deception and duplicity.
5. **Refrain from Taking Intoxicating Drinks and Drugs**: Intoxicants cloud the mind, leading to loss of control, poor judgment, and irresponsible behaviour. By refraining from intoxicants, we maintain a clear and focused mind, which is essential for developing wisdom and concentration. For example, choosing not to drink alcohol ensures that we remain mindful and aware, capable of making wise decisions. This precept helps us develop a mind that is free from delusion and mental confusion.

## The Importance of Precepts in Spiritual Development

The Five Precepts serve as a foundation for ethical conduct, which is necessary for the development of concentration and wisdom. When we break these precepts, our minds become agitated, disturbed by feelings of guilt, fear, and regret. Such a disturbed mind is incapable of attaining the deep concentration and insight required for enlightenment.

For example, consider someone who engages in lying or deceit. They may constantly worry about being caught, or they may experience inner turmoil as they try to maintain their falsehoods. This mental agitation prevents them from achieving the calm and focused mind needed for meditation. On the other hand, by upholding the precepts, we cultivate a mind that is peaceful, clear, and ready to engage in deeper spiritual practices.

The precepts also help us avoid actions that would lead to negative karmic consequences, both in this life and in future existences. By refraining from harmful actions, we create positive karma, which supports our progress on the path to liberation. Moreover, living according to the precepts helps us cultivate positive qualities such as compassion, integrity, and mindfulness, which are essential for spiritual development.

**Conclusion**

Taking refuge in the Lord Buddha, the Dhamma, and the Sangha is the first step on the path to liberation. It establishes a firm foundation of faith and trust that guides us through the challenges and temptations of the spiritual journey. Without this refuge, we are vulnerable to deviating from the path and becoming entangled in the endless cycle of craving and suffering.

The Five Precepts provide the ethical foundation necessary for spiritual growth. By committing to these precepts, we create the conditions for a peaceful and focused mind, free from the disturbances of unethical behaviour. This ethical conduct supports our practice of meditation and the development of wisdom, ultimately leading to the attainment of Nibbana.

In embracing the refuge of the Triple Gem and living according to the Five Precepts, we align ourselves with the path that leads to true liberation. We gradually overcome the obstacles that hinder our progress and move closer to the ultimate goal of complete freedom from suffering.

# 18
# Meditation:
## *The Path to Liberation and Ecstasy*

Meditation is a powerful tool that leads to liberation and the profound ecstasy that transcends ordinary human experience. It is not just a practice for calming the mind but a transformative process that guides us towards the ultimate goal of Nibbana, the cessation of suffering. Through meditation, we can penetrate the illusion of self and existence, gaining insight into the true nature of reality. In the Buddhist tradition, there are two primary types of meditation: Samatha (tranquilizing meditation) and Vipassana (insight meditation). Each of these meditative paths offers a unique approach to overcoming the illusions that bind us to the cycle of birth, suffering, and death.

**Samatha Meditation: Tranquilizing the Mind**

Samatha, or tranquilizing meditation, is a practice where the meditator focuses on a single object to calm the mind, achieving deep states of concentration known as Jhana. By repeatedly contemplating the object, whether it be the breath, a mantra, or a visual object, the mind gradually lets go of distractions and enters a state of profound stillness. This tranquility is not merely the absence of thought but a deeply peaceful state that brings transcendental happiness and ecstasy.

In this state of Jhana, the mind is so absorbed in the object of meditation that the sense of self temporarily dissolves. The meditator experiences joy and bliss that are far beyond the ordinary pleasures of the world. However, while Samatha can bring deep happiness and tranquility, it is not the end goal in itself. It serves as a powerful foundation for the more advanced practice of Vipassana, where insight into the nature of reality is cultivated.

**Vipassana Meditation: Gaining Insight into Reality**

Vipassana, or insight meditation, is the practice of directly observing the true nature of phenomena. Unlike Samatha, which focuses on calming the mind, Vipassana aims to develop wisdom by seeing things as they truly are. This type of meditation leads to the realization that the self and the world are mere illusions, freeing the meditator from attachment and leading to liberation.

Vipassana meditation involves observing the five clinging aggregates (form, sensation, perception, mental formations, and consciousness) that we mistakenly identify as the self. Through this practice, the meditator begins to see that these aggregates are impermanent, unsatisfactory, and non-self. By deeply understanding these truths, the mind naturally inclines towards letting go of attachment, leading to the stilling of all mental formations and the attainment of Nibbana.

There are three primary approaches to meditative enlightenment, each offering a different path to liberation:

1. **Tranquilizing the Mind First, Then Gaining Insight**

   The first approach involves starting with Samatha meditation to tranquilize the mind, followed by Vipassana to gain insight into the nature of reality. This method is accessible to all practitioners but requires significant time, effort, and dedication. The meditator first develops deep concentration by focusing on a single object until reaching the state of Jhana. After emerging from this deep absorption, the meditator then turns their attention to the five clinging aggregates, examining them with insight. This deep contemplation leads to the understanding that these aggregates are not self, culminating in the stilling of all mental formations and the realization of Nibbana.

   This path, while effective, can be challenging as it requires the meditator to maintain strong concentration before moving on to insight. However, for those who persist, it is a sure way to attain liberation.

2. **Gaining Insight First, Then Tranquilizing the Mind**

The second approach is considered the most effective for those with a natural affinity for understanding the Dhamma. This method begins with Vipassana meditation, where the practitioner gains insight into the true nature of reality right from the start. Through various insight patterns, such as contemplating the five clinging aggregates, seeing the world as mere name-and-form, or understanding the world through the six sense bases, etc, the meditator quickly penetrates the illusions of self and existence.

Once the mind has been emptied of delusion through insight, it naturally and effortlessly enters into the tranquil states of Jhana. This approach is particularly favored by those with keen wisdom and understanding, as it allows for a rapid progression towards liberation. As a meditation master, I also recommend this approach for many of my disciples, as it combines both insight and tranquility in a harmonious balance, leading to the swift realization of Nibbana.

### 3. Tranquilizing and Gaining Insight Simultaneously

The third approach involves practicing Samatha and Vipassana together, using techniques that simultaneously develop concentration and insight. Meditations such as the six sense bases awareness meditation or the 16 steps of Anapanasati meditation (mindfulness of breathing) are examples of this approach. In these practices, the meditator cultivates awareness of the present moment while also gaining insight into the impermanent, unsatisfactory, and non-self-nature of all phenomena.

This approach allows for a balanced development of both tranquillity and insight, leading to a more integrated and holistic experience of meditation. By simultaneously calming the mind and observing the true nature of reality, the meditator progresses steadily towards liberation.

## Conclusion

Meditation, whether through the tranquilizing practices of Samatha or the insightful practices of Vipassana, is the most effective and powerful tool for attaining liberation. By understanding the different approaches to meditation and choosing the one that resonates most with our own nature, we can move swiftly along the path to Nibbana. Whether through the gradual development of concentration followed by insight, the direct cultivation of wisdom leading to tranquility, or a balanced combination of both, meditation offers us the means to transcend the suffering of the world and experience the profound joy of liberation.

As we explore the different techniques and practices in the following chapters, remember that the ultimate goal of meditation is not just to find temporary peace or happiness, but to attain the lasting freedom that comes with the realization of Nibbana.

# 19
# Satipatthana:
## *The Four Bases of Mindfulness*

**Satipatthana** , often referred to as the Four Foundations or Bases of Mindfulness, is a profound practice in Buddhism that guides us toward the ultimate liberation by cultivating deep awareness and insight into the nature of reality. This practice involves observing and understanding the body, sensations, thoughts, and emotions in a manner that transcends ordinary experience. By engaging in this practice, we step back from our immediate identification with these phenomena, allowing us to see them as they truly are—impermanent, unsatisfactory, and non-self. This chapter explores each of these four bases of mindfulness in depth, providing practical guidance on how to cultivate them and the transformative effects they have on the path to enlightenment.

1. **Observing the Body: The First Base of Mindfulness**

The first foundation of mindfulness is the body. In this practice, we begin by observing the physical form, not as an identity or self, but as an object that can be seen, felt, and experienced. The body is often the most accessible object of meditation, as it is tangible and directly perceivable.

Start by sitting comfortably with a straight spine. Close your eyes and bring your attention to your body. Begin by observing your posture from head to toe and then from toe to head, as if you are wiping it with a towel. Move your awareness through each part of your body, noticing how it feels in the present moment. Observe the sensation of your feet on the ground, the weight of your body on the seat, the rise and fall of your chest as you breathe. As you continue this practice, you will notice that the body is not a solid, unchanging entity but a collection of parts that can be observed individually or as a whole.

By observing the body in this way, you gradually reduce the illusion that the body is the self. The mind begins to relinquish its attachment to the body, leading to a profound sense of detachment and peace. As you continue this practice, you may reach a point where it feels as though you can no longer observe your posture because the mind has let go of its identification with the body. This experience brings a deep calm and tranquility, paving the way for deeper meditative insights.

2. **Observing Sensations: The Second Base of Mindfulness**

The second foundation of mindfulness is the observation of sensations. Sensations are the physical and emotional experiences we perceive as pleasant, unpleasant, or neutral. These sensations often drive our reactions and behaviors, leading us to cling to pleasure and avoid pain. However, through mindfulness, we learn to observe sensations without attachment, seeing them as transient and impersonal.

Consider a moment when someone says something hurtful to you. The immediate reaction might be an unpleasant sensation—perhaps a tightening in the chest or a sinking feeling in the stomach. Normally, we identify with this sensation, believing it to be part of who we are. However, through mindfulness, we can step back and simply observe the sensation as it arises and passes away. This practice reveals that sensations are not permanent and do not define us. They are merely a series of events that arise due to causes and conditions.

A useful analogy is the observation of a heart rate monitor. The monitor shows the heart rate rising and falling in response to various stimuli. Similarly, sensations fluctuate based on external and internal conditions. By observing them without attachment, we gain a mature understanding that sensations are not the self; they are just passing experiences. Over time, this understanding diminishes our reactivity and strengthens our equanimity.

### 3. Observing Thoughts: The Third Base of Mindfulness

The third foundation of mindfulness is the observation of thoughts. Our thoughts often dominate our awareness, creating narratives that shape our perceptions and actions. However, thoughts are just mental events, arising and passing away like clouds in the sky. By observing them without judgment, we can disentangle ourselves from the stories they create and see them for what they truly are.

Imagine watching a procession from the sidelines. As an observer, you can see the entire procession, its beauty and its flaws, without being a part of it. Similarly, when we observe our thoughts, we do so as an outsider, not an insider caught up in the drama of the mind. This detachment allows us to witness thoughts with compassion and without judgment, much like listening to a child's chatter—amusing, perhaps, but not to be taken too seriously.

In this practice, it's important to give the mind a "silent treatment." When we stop engaging with our thoughts, much like a husband deciding not to respond to his wife's daily scolding, the mind begins to quiet down. Over time, the gaps between thoughts widen, and the mind becomes increasingly still. This stillness is not just an absence of thought but a profound peace that arises from no longer being entangled in the mental noise.

### 4. Observing Moods and Emotions: The Fourth Base of Mindfulness

The fourth foundation of mindfulness is the observation of moods and emotions. Emotions like love, anger, sadness, or excitement often color our perception of reality, leading us to react in ways that reinforce our identification with them. However, by stepping back and observing these emotions as they arise, we can see them as transient states that do not define who we are.

For instance, consider the feeling of sleepiness. Instead of being overcome by it, you can observe it as a passing mood. Notice how it feels in your body and mind. Similarly, emotions like love or stress can be observed with the same detachment. By not becoming a participant in these emotions, you create a space between the emotion and your awareness. This space allows you to witness the emotion without being swept away by it.

Eventually, through this practice, the mind experiences a sense of emptiness—a void where emotions and moods no longer hold sway. However, even this emptiness should not be mistaken for the self. The observer, which seems to be a detached witness, is also a mental construct, a thought that is observing other thoughts. The final stage of mindfulness involves observing this observer itself, recognizing that even the observer is not the self. When this last identification dissolves, the mind becomes free from all mental formations and preparations, leading to a state of complete stillness and peace.

**The Experience of Initial Enlightenment**

This state of stillness, where all perceptions and sensations have ceased, is the experience of initial enlightenment, known as Sotapanna. A Sotapanna is one who has seen the path to liberation clearly and knows what real happiness is. This experience is the first glimpse of Nibbana, where the mind is completely free from the illusions of self and existence. It is the beginning of the end of suffering and the start of a journey towards full liberation.

In summary, the practice of Satipatthana—mindfulness of the body, sensations, thoughts, and emotions—leads us step by step to the realization of the impermanent, unsatisfactory, and non-self nature of all phenomena. By observing these aspects of our experience without attachment, we gradually loosen the bonds of ignorance and delusion, allowing us to move closer to the ultimate goal of liberation. Through persistent and mindful practice, we can all experience the profound peace and happiness that comes with true insight and enlightenment.

# 20
# The 16 Steps of Ānāpānasati: *A Comprehensive Guide to Breath Meditation*

**Ānāpānasati** , or mindfulness of breathing, is a meditation practice detailed in the Anapanasati Sutta from the Majjhima Nikaya of the Sutta Pitaka. Among various methods of breath awareness, the 16-step approach stands out as the most precise and comprehensive, as it was explicitly prescribed by Lord Buddha himself. This method integrates both Samatha (tranquillising meditation) and Vipassana (insight meditation) and is renowned for its effectiveness in leading practitioners to Nibbana (enlightenment) without requiring additional methods. This chapter elaborates on each of the 16 steps in detail, offering a step-by-step guide to this profound meditative practice.

**Preparing for Meditation**

Before delving into the 16 steps, it is crucial to prepare the body and mind. Find a quiet place, ideally a secluded spot in the wilderness, the shade of a tree, or a serene room. Sit down with your legs folded crosswise, ensuring that your back is straight and your body is erect. Set mindfulness to the forefront of your practice, establishing a strong foundation for the meditation.

**Step 1: Understanding the Long Breath**

Begin by directing your awareness to the breath. When you inhale, discern whether the breath is long. Recognise it as such by noting, "I am breathing in long." This initial step involves simply acknowledging the length of the breath without judgement.

**Step 2: Understanding the Short Breath**

Similarly, as you exhale, determine if the breath is short. Label it as such with the awareness, "I am breathing out short." Just as a carpenter can tell the length of each stroke before beginning, so should you recognise whether each breath is long or short from the beginning of the inhale or exhale.

**Step 3: Experiencing the Whole Body with the Breath**

In this step, extend your awareness to encompass the entire body as you breathe in. Observe how the breath permeates through the body. Similarly, as you breathe out, experience the breath leaving the body. This practice helps in connecting the breath with bodily sensations, fostering a holistic awareness.

**Step 4: Tranquillising the Breath**

Focus on calming the bodily sensations associated with the breath. As you breathe in, train yourself to calm the bodily fabrications (calming the breathing and the physical sensations related to breathing). Likewise, as you exhale, continue to calm these bodily fabrications. This step is about achieving a state of tranquillity through the breath.

**Step 5: Experiencing Rapture**

Direct your awareness to the experience of rapture or joy that accompanies the breath. As you breathe in, become sensitive to the rapture, and as you breathe out, continue to be aware of it. This step involves cultivating a sense of joy and bliss that arises through mindful breathing.

**Step 6: Experiencing Pleasure**

Similarly, focus on the pleasure derived from the breath. While breathing in, be aware of the pleasurable sensations, and as you breathe out, continue to experience this pleasure. This step aims to enhance your sensitivity to the pleasure that arises through the practice.

**Step 7: Understanding Mental Fabrication**

Recognise that mental fabrications—such as perceptions and sensations—are part of the cycle of experience. As you breathe in, be aware of these fabrications, and as you breathe out, continue to observe them. Understanding that even pleasurable sensations are fabrications helps in developing insight into the nature of mental formations.

**Step 8: Calming Mental Fabrication**

Train yourself to calm the mental fabrications as you breathe in and out. By recognising that perceptions and sensations are transient, you work towards calming these mental fabrications, fostering a state of inner peace and equanimity.

**Step 9: Observing the Mind**

Direct your awareness to the state of the mind itself. As you breathe in, be sensitive to the mind's state, and as you breathe out, maintain this awareness. This step involves becoming attuned to the mind's emptiness and overall state.

**Step 10: Satisfying the Mind**

Focus on satisfying the mind with each breath. As you inhale, intentionally bring satisfaction to the mind, and as you exhale, continue to sustain this satisfaction. This practice aims to cultivate a sense of contentment and joy within the mind.

**Step 11: Steadying the Mind**

Work on steadying the mind as you breathe in and out. As you inhale, focus on steadying the mind and, likewise, as you exhale, continue to stabilise it. This step helps in maintaining mental focus and clarity.

**Step 12: Releasing the Mind**

Train yourself to release the mind from the state of consciousness experienced. While breathing in, focus on releasing the mind, and as you breathe out, continue to disengage from the current state of consciousness. This practice involves stepping back from the present mental state rather than relinquishing consciousness itself.

**Step 13: Focusing on Inconstancy**

Observe the inconstancy of the mind as you breathe in and out. Recognise how the state of consciousness changes with each breath. This awareness of inconstancy helps in understanding the impermanent nature of all phenomena.

**Step 14: Focusing on Dispassion**

Develop a sense of dispassion or fading towards the consciousness experienced. As you breathe in, focus on becoming detached from the current state of consciousness, and as you exhale, continue to cultivate dispassion. This step helps in recognising the transient nature of all experiences.

**Step 15: Focusing on Cessation**

Direct your attention to the cessation of consciousness. As you inhale, observe how the state of consciousness you experience is not the same as it was moments ago or will be in the future. This focus on cessation helps in understanding the fleeting nature of all mental states.

**Step 16: Focusing on Relinquishment**

Finally, focus on relinquishing the current state of consciousness as you breathe in and out. Recognise that after observing cessation, you need to relinquish the consciousness you are experiencing now. This step involves releasing attachment to the current state of consciousness, leading to a deeper sense of freedom.

**The Experience of Nibbana**

Upon completing these 16 steps, the mind will naturally settle and cease all preparatory activity. You will reach a state where there is no perception of breathing or consciousness, allowing for a direct experience of Nibbana. This profound state marks the initial realisation of enlightenment, where the mind is freed from all attachments and fabrications.

**Conclusion**

The 16 steps of Anapanasati offer a structured and comprehensive approach to breath meditation that incorporates both tranquillising and insight practices. By following these steps meticulously, practitioners can cultivate a deep understanding of the impermanent and non-self-nature of all phenomena, ultimately leading to the experience of Nibbana. This method, as prescribed by Lord Buddha, provides a complete and effective path to liberation through the art of mindful breathing.

# 21
# Steps to Attain Liberation:
## *Relinquishing the Five Clinging Aggregates*

Attaining liberation, or Nibbana, necessitates a profound understanding and relinquishment of the five clinging aggregates (khandhas) — form (body), feeling (sensations), perception, mental formations (sankharas), and consciousness. This chapter elucidates the sequential process required to transcend these aggregates and achieve the cessation of all preparatory activities, culminating in the realisation of Nibbana.

### 1. Relinquishing the Body

The first step in the journey towards liberation involves understanding the nature of the body. Recognise that the body is not the self or soul, but merely a mechanism, akin to a machine. Despite any meditation method employed, the realisation must dawn that the body is an aggregate of physical processes and not an intrinsic self.

By relinquishing the notion that the body constitutes the self, the mind may initially experience a calm state. This tranquillity, however, may lead to a mistaken belief that it represents the self. One must persist in recognising that this calm state is also not the self, but a transient phenomenon arising from perceptions and sensations, which themselves are impermanent.

2. **Understanding Perceptions and Sensations**

Once the body is relinquished as a sense of self, the mind tends to become entangled with perceptions and sensations. It is crucial to comprehend that these perceptions and sensations are also mechanisms rather than a permanent self.

This understanding leads to the recognition that even the calm state, which might initially seem like the self, is a cycle of arising and passing away sensations. By observing the impermanent nature of perceptions and sensations, one further disentangles from the belief that these are the self.

3. **Relinquishing Consciousness**

After relinquishing the perceptions and sensations, the mind might start identifying with the state of consciousness itself. It is essential to discern that consciousness, too, is not a singular, permanent entity or soul.

Consciousness arises and passes away based on causes and conditions, such as name and form (nama-rupa). By understanding that consciousness is also a transient process rather than an immutable self, one continues the journey towards relinquishment.

### 4. Realising the Emptiness of Mind

Upon relinquishing consciousness, a profound sense of pure emptiness may be experienced. At this stage, it is vital to comprehend that even this state of emptiness is not a permanent self or soul. The mind may again cling to the emptiness, mistaking it for an enduring self.

Recognise that the state of emptiness is also impermanent and will cease after a certain period. If one were truly the emptiness, then the cessation of emptiness would imply the cessation of the self. Thus, emptiness, too, must be relinquished as it is also impermanent and devoid of self.

### 5. Understanding the Nature of Nibbana

The final realisation is the complete cessation of all preparatory activities. When the mind has relinquished the aggregates — body, sensations, perceptions, and consciousness — one experiences the state of Nibbana. At this point, all clinging and attachment have ceased, and the mind is fully liberated from all fabrications.

**The Differences Between Emptiness and Nibbana**

The distinction between the state of emptiness and Nibbana is subtle yet significant. In the state of emptiness, perceptions are still operating in a subtle manner, and there is still an observer who experiences this state. However, in Nibbana, there is no observer, and the perception of emptiness or calmness ceases. The experience of Nibbana is characterised by a complete cessation of all preparatory activities and the total absence of any perceiving self.

**Experiential Descriptions of the Stilling of Preparations**

Practitioners who have reached the state of stillness often describe their experiences in various ways. Some may liken it to sinking into a deep well, with each relinquishment of the aggregates feeling like a gradual descent into deeper and deeper levels of selflessness. Others might describe the sensation as if a massive rock has been placed upon their head, bringing the mind to a complete halt. Still, others speak of travelling through a vast tunnel, eventually reaching a blind wall, symbolising the final cessation of all attachments.

These descriptions reflect the deeply personal and unique experiences of individuals as they approach the profound stillness of Nibbana. Each practitioner may perceive this process differently, but the common thread remains the complete relinquishment of all forms of self and preparation.

**Conclusion**

The path to liberation involves a meticulous process of relinquishing the five clinging aggregates. By recognising that each aggregate — body, sensations, perceptions, mental formations, and consciousness — is impermanent and not the self, practitioners can gradually attain the stilling of all preparations. This culminates in the profound realisation of Nibbana, where all fabrications and perceptions cease, and the mind experiences ultimate freedom. Understanding these steps in detail provides a clear and structured approach to the profound journey of attaining liberation.

# 22
# The Five Clinging Aggregates:
## *An Illusion of Self and the Path to Insight*

In Buddhism, the notion of self is often examined through the lens of the five aggregates (pañcakkhandhā), also referred to as the "five clinging aggregates" (pañcupādānakkhandhā). These aggregates, or components of existence, are: form (rūpa), feeling (vedanā), perception (saññā), fabrications or volitional activities (saṅkhārā), and consciousness (viññāṇa). Together, they form the foundation of what we experience as "self." However, the Buddha taught that these aggregates are not self, but rather impermanent and subject to change. Understanding their illusory nature is key to breaking free from suffering and realizing Nibbāna.

To illustrate this, the Buddha used vivid metaphors to describe the illusory and insubstantial nature of the five aggregates. In this chapter, we will explore these metaphors and their deeper meaning, showing how they reveal the aggregates to be like illusions—empty of essence and yet deceptively convincing.

### 1. Form (Rūpa) as a Lump of Foam

The aggregate of form refers to the physical body and all material phenomena. It includes everything that we perceive as solid, tangible, and substantial—our body, the objects we encounter, and the material world. In daily life, we tend to regard form as solid and permanent, a foundation upon which we build our sense of identity. However, the Buddha likened form to a lump of foam, which may appear substantial from a distance but is in reality empty and insubstantial.

Imagine a lump of foam floating on the surface of a river. From afar, it might seem like a solid mass, but upon closer inspection, it is revealed to be nothing more than bubbles, with no true substance inside. In the same way, the body and physical world seem solid, but upon investigation, they are seen as impermanent, constantly changing, and ultimately empty of any enduring self. The body is made up of cells, which are made up of atoms, and on a deeper level, even atoms are mostly empty space.

The lump of foam metaphor challenges our deeply ingrained belief in the solidity of our physical existence. Just as foam can dissipate in an instant, so too can the body and all material phenomena disappear, leaving no trace of solidity. This recognition is essential for loosening our attachment to form as part of our identity.

### 2. Feeling (Vedanā) as a Bubble

Feeling refers to the sensations of pleasure, pain, and neutrality that arise in response to contact with the world. Whether we are enjoying a delicious meal, feeling the discomfort of illness, or experiencing the neutrality of an everyday moment, feelings play a central role in shaping our reactions and attachments. However, the Buddha described feeling as being like a bubble.

Consider the nature of a bubble: it arises suddenly, floats for a brief moment, and then bursts, disappearing without a trace. Feelings, too, are fleeting. They arise, remain for a short time, and then pass away. Yet, despite their transitory nature, we often cling to feelings, craving pleasurable sensations and trying to avoid painful ones. This attachment leads to suffering because feelings, like bubbles, cannot last.

When we examine feelings closely, we begin to see that they are impermanent, insubstantial, and beyond our control. Just as bubbles are delicate and ephemeral, feelings come and go without leaving anything enduring behind. By understanding this, we can learn to let go of our attachment to feelings and no longer be swayed by the constant ebb and flow of pleasure and pain.

### 3. Perception (Saññā) as a Mirage

Perception is the mental process that allows us to recognize and categorize the objects and experiences we encounter. It is through perception that we label things as "pleasant," "unpleasant," "tree," "person," or "birdsong." However, perception is not always accurate—it is shaped by our conditioning, beliefs, and expectations. The Buddha compared perception to a mirage.

A mirage appears to be real, but it is an optical illusion. From a distance, one might see what seems to be water shimmering in the desert, but upon closer examination, it becomes clear that there is no water at all. Perception operates in a similar way. We may perceive things to be solid, permanent, and substantial, but these perceptions are often illusions created by the mind.

For example, when we perceive someone as being a source of happiness or a source of suffering, we may not be seeing them as they truly are. Our perceptions are coloured by our past experiences, desires, and fears, leading us to mistake the appearance of reality for reality itself. By recognizing perception as a mirage, we can begin to loosen our attachment to the labels and judgments we place on the world and see things more clearly, as they truly are—impermanent and without inherent essence.

### 4. Fabrications (Saṅkhārā) as Searching for a Stem in a Banana Tree

Fabrications, or volitional activities, are the mental formations that shape our intentions and actions. They include thoughts, emotions, desires, and the underlying tendencies that drive our behavior. The Buddha described fabrications as being like searching for a stem in a banana tree.

When we peel away the layers of a banana tree, expecting to find a solid core or stem, we are left with nothing. There is no central stem—only layer upon layer of soft, fibrous material. In the same way, when we examine the volitional activities of the mind, we find that they are not grounded in anything substantial. Our thoughts, emotions, and intentions arise in response to conditions, but there is no solid "self" behind them.

Fabrications are a process of mental conditioning, constantly arising and passing away in response to stimuli. They may seem to define us—"I am a kind person," "I am an angry person," "I want this," "I don't want that"—but upon investigation, we see that they are just patterns of thought and behavior, not an enduring self. Like the banana tree, fabrications are empty at their core. By recognizing this, we can begin to loosen our attachment to the mental activities that drive our suffering.

### 5. Consciousness (Viññāṇa) as a Magic Trick

Consciousness is the awareness of sensory experiences—sight, sound, smell, taste, touch, and thought. It is through consciousness that we become aware of the world and our inner experiences. However, the Buddha compared consciousness to a magic trick, which creates the illusion of duality—an independently existing world and an independent observer.

Just as a magician can deceive us into believing in something that isn't really there, consciousness deceives us into believing in a duality between "me" and "the world." When we hear the sound of a bird, consciousness creates the illusion that there is an independently existing bird and an independently existing "me" who hears it. In reality, this duality is a thought that arises after the consciousness of sound has already occurred.

Consciousness, like a magic trick, presents a world of seeming reality, but upon close examination, we see that this world is an illusion created by the mind. The bird and the self that hears it do not exist independently of consciousness. They are part of the same process of awareness. By understanding consciousness as a magic trick, we can begin to unravel the illusion of duality and see through the false sense of separation between "self" and "world."

**The Illusion of Self**

Taken together, the five aggregates—form, feeling, perception, fabrications, and consciousness—create the illusion of a permanent, independent self. We identify with our body, our sensations, our perceptions, our thoughts, and our awareness, believing them to be "me." But upon closer examination, we see that these aggregates are like foam, bubbles, mirages, banana trees, and magic tricks—empty of any inherent substance.

By understanding the true nature of the five aggregates, we can begin to see through the illusion of self and loosen our attachment to the things we mistakenly believe to be permanent and real. This insight is the key to breaking free from suffering and realizing the profound peace of Nibbāna. The aggregates are impermanent, conditioned, and empty of self—realizing this truth is the path to liberation.

**Conclusion: Letting Go of Illusion**

The metaphors of foam, bubbles, mirages, banana trees, and magic tricks serve as powerful reminders that what we cling to as "self" is not what it appears to be. Form, feeling, perception, fabrications, and consciousness—all the components of our existence—are fleeting, insubstantial, and ultimately empty.

By deeply contemplating the nature of the five aggregates, we can begin to see through the illusions that keep us trapped in the cycle of suffering. We loosen our attachment to the body, sensations, perceptions, thoughts, and even consciousness itself, and in doing so, we open the door to true freedom—Nibbāna.

# 23
# The Posture of Meditation:
## *An Exploration of Proper Practice and Postural Variations*

Meditation, an essential practice for spiritual development and liberation, can be undertaken in various postures that accommodate individual needs and circumstances. Whether sitting, standing, walking, or lying down, maintaining proper posture during meditation is critical to ensuring a conducive environment for mental stillness and awareness. This chapter will explore the various postures suitable for meditation, including the significance of each, the importance of consistency, and the guidance provided by the Lord Buddha regarding daily meditation practices.

### 1. The Importance of Posture in Meditation

The posture adopted during meditation significantly impacts the quality of practice. A stable and comfortable posture allows the mind to settle, while discomfort or imbalance can become a distraction, pulling the attention away from the object of meditation. However, meditation is not restricted to one fixed position; instead, it offers flexibility, accommodating different physical capabilities and preferences.

## 2. Meditative Postures: Sitting, Standing, Walking, and Lying Down

### Sitting Meditation

Sitting is perhaps the most commonly associated posture with meditation. The traditional cross-legged position, often seen in statues of the Lord Buddha, is highly recommended for its stability and grounding effects. In this posture, the legs are crossed, with one foot resting on the opposite thigh (full lotus) or one foot resting on the opposite calf (half lotus). The hands are typically placed in the lap, with the right hand resting on the left, and the thumbs lightly touching.

For those who find the cross-legged position challenging or uncomfortable, sitting on a chair is a perfectly acceptable alternative. When seated on a chair, it is crucial to maintain a straight spine, ensuring that the back is not slouched. The chest should be pushed slightly forward, creating an open and upright posture, and the neck should be held slightly higher than usual, aligning with the spine. This alignment fosters a state of alertness and presence, reducing the likelihood of drowsiness or distraction.

**Standing Meditation**

Standing meditation, while less common, is another viable option, especially for those who may experience discomfort when sitting for extended periods. In standing meditation, the feet should be placed hip-width apart, with the weight evenly distributed across both feet. The knees should be slightly bent, avoiding any locking of the joints. The spine remains straight, with the chest open and the head held high, just as in the seated posture. Standing meditation can be particularly beneficial for cultivating mindfulness of the body and the sensations of balance and gravity.

**Walking Meditation**

Walking meditation offers a dynamic alternative to the stillness of sitting and standing meditation. This practice involves slow, deliberate movement, with full awareness placed on the sensations of each step. The walker moves with purpose, focusing on the lifting, moving, and placing of the feet. Walking meditation is a powerful practice for developing mindfulness in motion and is especially useful when the mind is too restless for sitting meditation. The key is to maintain a calm, focused awareness throughout the movement, allowing the mind to anchor in the present moment.

### Lying Down Meditation

Meditation can also be practiced while lying down, though this posture requires careful consideration to avoid falling asleep. The recommended position is lying on the right side in what is known as the "sinha seiya," or the lion's posture. This position, traditionally favoured by the Lord Buddha, involves lying with the right arm extended, supporting the head, and the left arm resting along the body. The legs are slightly bent, with the left leg resting on the right. This posture, while conducive to relaxation, still requires mindfulness to maintain awareness and prevent drowsiness.

## 3. The Significance of Consistency in Meditation Practice

The Lord Buddha emphasized the importance of regular meditation practice, advising that one should meditate at least three times a day, for approximately 30 minutes each session. This consistent practice helps to cultivate mindfulness and deepen concentration, gradually leading to greater insight and understanding.

However, it is recognised that modern life can pose challenges to maintaining such a rigorous schedule. If three sessions a day prove impossible, it is still beneficial to meditate twice daily. The key is not to allow the demands of daily life to entirely overshadow the practice of meditation. To ensure consistency, one may set an alarm to remind themselves to begin and end their meditation practice, making it a non-negotiable part of the daily routine.

### 4. Making Meditation Accessible: Practical Tips for Daily Practice

For those struggling to find time for meditation, integrating it into the daily schedule is vital. By setting aside specific times each day, whether early in the morning, during a lunch break, or before bedtime, meditation becomes a habitual practice, no different from other essential daily activities.

It is important to start with a realistic commitment, gradually increasing the time and frequency as the practice becomes more ingrained. Even if the initial sessions are brief, the consistency of practice will build a strong foundation for deeper meditation in the future. The use of a timer or alarm ensures that the meditation period is adhered to, preventing the mind from becoming restless or overly focused on the passage of time.

### 5. Avoiding Common Pitfalls in Meditation Posture

One of the most common challenges in meditation is maintaining a proper posture without succumbing to discomfort or drowsiness. If seated meditation becomes uncomfortable, it is advisable to adjust the posture slightly rather than endure pain or strain, which can become a distraction. The body's comfort is essential for the mind to relax and focus.

Another pitfall is the tendency to slouch or slump, especially when tired. This not only affects the physical posture but also leads to mental dullness. Regular checks on posture, ensuring the spine is straight and the chest open, can help maintain alertness and prevent the mind from becoming sluggish.

### 6. Adapting Meditation to Individual Needs

Each individual may have different needs and limitations, and meditation practice should be adapted accordingly. Whether due to age, health conditions, or personal preference, the posture should be chosen based on what allows for the most comfortable and focused practice. The flexibility of meditation postures ensures that everyone, regardless of physical ability, can engage in this transformative practice.

## Conclusion

The posture of meditation is not merely a physical alignment but a crucial element that supports the mental focus and clarity necessary for deep practice. By understanding the different postures available — sitting, standing, walking, and lying down — and their respective benefits, practitioners can choose the most suitable method for their circumstances. The guidance of the Lord Buddha, emphasizing the importance of regular practice, reminds us of the necessity of integrating meditation into our daily lives. Whether meditating three times a day or adapting to a more feasible schedule, the key lies in consistency, mindfulness, and a commitment to the path of liberation.

# 24
# Anichcha Anupassana:
## *Discerning Impermanence Meditation*

In the journey toward liberation, understanding the true nature of reality is essential. Among the insights that lead to this understanding, discerning impermanence (Anicca Anupassana) holds a pivotal role. This chapter will guide you through an insight meditation that helps to deeply observe and comprehend the impermanent nature of the five clinging aggregates—body, sensations, perceptions, volitional activities, and consciousness. By methodically discerning these elements, one gradually loosens the attachment to them, ultimately leading to the realization of their non-self-nature and the experience of emptiness.

**Preparing for Meditation**

Before beginning the meditation, choose a comfortable posture. You may sit, stand, or even walk, ensuring your spine is straight and your body relaxed. Close your eyes and prepare your mind to deeply observe the truths of impermanence. Throughout this practice, maintain mindful awareness, focusing entirely on the present moment as you explore each aggregate.

### 1. Discerning the Impermanence of the Body

Start by reflecting on the impermanence of your own body. Visualize the different stages of your life:

- **Infancy**: Remember how small and delicate your body was.
- **Preschool and School Years**: Recall the changes as you grew, the physical transformations during childhood.
- **Teenage Years**: Reflect on the changes during adolescence—your body's growth, the emergence of new physical characteristics.
- **Young Adulthood**: Consider how your body developed further into adulthood.
- **Middle Age**: Notice the ongoing changes that occur as the body ages.

Progress further by contemplating the changes that occurred over shorter periods:

- **Two Years Ago, One Year Ago**: Notice how your body has continued to change even within the last few years.
- **Last Month, Last Week**: Reflect on the more recent, subtle changes.
- **Yesterday, This Morning, Five Minutes Ago**: Observe the continuous, ongoing transformation.

With each reflection, understand that the body has always been in a state of flux. Now, look to the future:

- **Tomorrow, Next Month, Next Year**: Realize that these changes will continue. Your body will age, and eventually, it will decay. Imagine yourself many years from now, perhaps even as a skeleton in a grave.

Finally, focus on the present moment. Recognize that this very body, which has changed in the past and will continue to change in the future, is also changing right now. By giving full attention to the constant changing of your body, you will begin to experience its impermanence directly.

2. **Discerning the Impermanence of Loved Ones**

Next, apply this same discernment to the bodies of your loved ones:

- **Your Mother, Father, and Beloved Ones**: Reflect on their physical changes over time, from infancy to their current state. Understand that their bodies are also in a constant state of flux, just like yours. Acknowledge the present moment, recognizing that their bodies, too, are changing right now.

3. **Discerning the Impermanence of Material Things**

Extend this discernment to material objects around you:

- **Tables, Watches, Homes, Villages**: These seemingly solid and permanent objects are also subject to change. Imagine the wear and tear that has occurred over the years, and how these objects will continue to deteriorate. Bring your awareness to the present, and feel the subtle changes happening even now.

4. **Discerning the Impermanence of Sensations**

Now, turn your attention to sensations—both pleasant and unpleasant:

- **Past Sensations**: Reflect on the most pleasant sensation you've ever experienced; it has completely vanished. The most unpleasant sensation is also gone. Even neutral sensations, neither pleasant nor unpleasant, have faded away. Recall sensations from yesterday, this morning, or even a minute ago—they, too, have ceased.

Consider the future:

- **Future Sensations**: Whether it's the touch of a loved one or the pain of an injury, these sensations will also vanish. Understand that every sensation, no matter how intense, is impermanent.

Finally, bring your focus to the present moment:

- **Present Sensations**: Realize that the sensations you are experiencing right now are also changing. Deeply understand this as you experience it, observing the impermanence of all sensations through sounds, tangibles and thoughts.

5. **Discerning the Impermanence of Perceptions**

Next, contemplate the impermanence of perceptions:

- **Past Perceptions**: Good and bad perceptions from the past have ceased. Recall perceptions from yesterday, this morning, or even a few minutes ago—they have all vanished.

Now, consider the future:

- **Future Perceptions**: In the next 30 seconds, the perception you are holding will change. In 10 hours, tomorrow, or 10 years from now, your perceptions will continue to change.

Focus on the present moment:

- **Present Perceptions**: Observe how your perceptions, arising from sounds, tangibles, and thoughts, are constantly shifting. Experience the impermanence of perceptions as they change from moment to moment.
-

6. **Discerning the Impermanence of Volitional Activities**

Now, turn your attention to volitional activities, such as thoughts:

- **Past Thoughts**: Thoughts from your childhood, adolescence, and even your best or worst thoughts have all ceased. Recall yesterday's thoughts, this morning's thoughts, or those from a minute ago—they have all vanished.

Consider the future:

- **Future Thoughts**: Understand that future thoughts, whether they are thoughts of anger, lust, or anything else, will also cease. Imagine yourself in the future—every thought you will have is destined to vanish, just like those in the past.

Focus on the present moment:

- **Present Volitional Activities**: Observe how every volitional activity is also changing right now. Experience the impermanence of your thoughts and mental activities as they arise and pass away.

### 7. Discerning the Impermanence of Consciousness

Finally, contemplate the impermanence of consciousness:

- **Past Consciousnesses**: Recall past moments of consciousness—when someone loved you, blamed you, or touched you—these moments of awareness have all ceased.

Consider the future:

- **Future Consciousnesses**: Whatever experiences will arise in the future, whether they are pleasant or unpleasant, they too will change and cease. Imagine the consciousness you will have tomorrow, next year, or in old age—they are all subject to the same impermanent nature.

Focus on the present moment:

- **Present Consciousness**: Observe the subtle changes in your consciousness right now. Watch as your experience of awareness shifts from moment to moment, revealing its impermanent nature. If you're finding it difficult to perceive these changes, gently pose a question to your mind: "Is this consciousness the same as the consciousness I experienced just three seconds ago? Will it be the same as the consciousness I will experience three seconds from now?" As you ask these questions, allow your mind to respond naturally. You'll begin to realize, with a deep sense of understanding, that consciousness is not a static entity—it is constantly changing, moment by moment. This realization helps to reveal the impermanent nature of consciousness, guiding you toward a clearer understanding of its transient nature.

As you deeply observe the impermanence of consciousness, you may find yourself entering a state of emptiness.

### 8. Discerning the Impermanence of Emptiness

Even the state of emptiness is not immune to impermanence:

- **Impermanence of Emptiness**: Understand that this state of emptiness, no matter how profound, will also change. If you cling to this emptiness as "I am," recognize that when the emptiness ceases, the self you identify with it must also cease. Discern this emptiness as non-self and let it go.

By discerning the impermanence of even emptiness, you will enter the state of stilling all preparations—Nibbana.

**Conclusion**

Through the practice of Anicca Anupassana, you systematically observe and understand the impermanence of the five clinging aggregates. This deep insight gradually loosens the mind's attachment to these aggregates, leading to the realization that they are not self. By relinquishing these attachments, one moves closer to the experience of emptiness and ultimately, the stilling of all preparations—Nibbana. This meditation is a powerful tool on the path to liberation, helping you to see the world as it truly is: a constantly changing, impermanent phenomenon devoid of any permanent self.

# 25
# Dukkha Anupassana:
## *Discerning the Suffering of Existence*

"Dukkha Anupassana," or the discernment of suffering, is a profound meditation practice focused on recognizing the inherent suffering within the five aggregates: body, sensations, perceptions, volitional activities, and consciousness. This practice helps us understand that these aggregates are not merely temporary but are fundamentally sources of ongoing stress and discomfort. Through this realization, we can attain liberation from clinging and ultimately reach a state of profound peace.

**Preparation for Meditation:** To start, find a quiet, comfortable space where you will not be disturbed. Sit or stand with a straight spine, ensuring that your posture is both relaxed and alert. Close your eyes and align your chest slightly forward, with your neck gently elevated. This posture helps maintain focus and awareness throughout the meditation.

1. **The Body: The Root of Persistent Suffering**

**Reflection on the Body:**

- **Past Suffering:** Reflect on how the body has been a source of suffering in both this life and past lives. Recall specific experiences of physical pain and discomfort: the agony of a prolonged illness, the distress from an injury, or the limitations caused by chronic conditions. Recognize that these past experiences stem from having a body.
- **Future Suffering:** Envision the suffering that may arise from the body in the future. Consider potential ailments and accidents that could occur: chronic diseases like arthritis, the pain of aging, or the impact of an unexpected injury. Visualize these scenarios and understand that they represent future sources of suffering.
- **Present Suffering:** Examine how your body is currently a source of suffering. Focus on any present discomforts, such as aches, pains, or physical limitations. Recognize that even now, the body is contributing to your suffering.

Acknowledge and deeply understand: "I relinquish! I relinquish!" Recognize that the body, as an aggregate, is fundamentally tied to suffering. Relinquish clinging to the body, understanding that its very existence is a source of ongoing stress and discomfort.

2. **Sensations: The Ever-Changing Source of Discomfort**

**Reflection on Sensations:**

- **Past Sensations:** Reflect on the range of sensations you have experienced in the past. Both pleasant and unpleasant sensations have come and gone, leaving behind a trail of suffering. For example, consider how the pleasure from a delightful meal eventually faded, or how the discomfort from a past injury has now passed but was significant while it lasted.
- **Future Sensations:** Anticipate future sensations and their potential to cause suffering. Envision how future experiences of pleasure or pain will arise and eventually wane. For instance, imagine the joy of a future event that will eventually lead to disappointment or the anticipated discomfort from a future illness.
- **Present Sensations:** Focus on the sensations you are experiencing right now. Recognize how every sensation, whether pleasant or unpleasant, is fleeting and contributes to your stress. For example, the temporary comfort of your current sitting position may soon turn into discomfort.

Acknowledge and deeply understand: "I relinquish! I relinquish!" Recognize that sensations, in their transient nature, are a constant source of suffering. Relinquish clinging to sensations, understanding that their very existence is tied to ongoing discomfort and stress.

### 3. Perceptions: The Source of Distress Through Changing Views

**Reflection on Perceptions:**

- **Past Perceptions:** Reflect on the perceptions you held in the past. These perceptions, whether positive or negative, have changed and contributed to your suffering. For example, consider how your perception of a once-cherished experience or person has shifted, leading to disappointment or dissatisfaction.
- **Future Perceptions:** Envision future perceptions and their potential to cause suffering. Anticipate how your views and judgments about people, events, or situations will evolve, potentially leading to future distress. For instance, think about how the idealization of future relationships or achievements may lead to eventual disillusionment.
- **Present Perceptions:** Focus on your current perceptions. Recognize how they are constantly changing and often contribute to stress. For example, consider how your perception of your current environment or relationships may shift, causing you distress.

Acknowledge and deeply understand: "I relinquish! I relinquish!" Recognize that perceptions, in their ever-changing nature, are a source of ongoing distress. Relinquish clinging to perceptions, understanding that their existence is tied to suffering and discomfort.

### 4. Volitional Activities: The Source of Mental Stress

**Reflection on Volitional Activities:**

- **Past Thoughts:** Reflect on the thoughts and intentions you have had in the past. These thoughts, whether positive or negative, have caused suffering and stress. For example, consider the mental anguish from past anxieties or regrets that have lingered.
- **Future Thoughts:** Anticipate future thoughts and their potential to cause suffering. Envision how future worries, fears, or desires will contribute to mental stress. For instance, think about the anticipated stress from future career uncertainties or personal relationships.
- **Present Thoughts:** Focus on the thoughts and intentions you are experiencing right now. Recognize how they contribute to your mental stress and suffering. For example, consider how obsessive or fearful thoughts are causing you ongoing discomfort.

Acknowledge and deeply understand: "I relinquish! I relinquish!" Recognize that volitional activities, in their constant flux, are a source of mental stress. Relinquish clinging to thoughts and intentions, understanding that they are inherently tied to suffering.

5. **Consciousness: The Ever-Changeable Source of Distress**

**Reflection on Consciousness:**

- **Past Consciousness:** Reflect on past states of consciousness. Recognize how your awareness of past experiences has contributed to suffering. For example, the consciousness of past joys or sorrows has led to ongoing distress.
- **Future Consciousness:** Contemplate future states of consciousness and their potential to cause suffering. Envision how future experiences of awareness will lead to distress. For instance, think about how future fears or anxieties will impact your consciousness.
- **Present Consciousness:** Observe the subtle changes in your consciousness right now. Recognize how your awareness is constantly shifting and contributing to stress. For example, consider how your current state of awareness of your surroundings or thoughts is perpetually changing.
-

Acknowledge and deeply understand: "I relinquish! I relinquish!" Recognize that consciousness, in its ever-changing nature, is a source of ongoing distress. Relinquish clinging to consciousness, understanding that it is tied to suffering and discomfort.

**Attaining Emptiness and Liberation**

**Achieving Emptiness:**
After thoroughly discerning the suffering within these five aggregates, your mind may naturally move toward experiencing the state of emptiness. This state arises when you fully recognize the inherent suffering in all aggregates. However, if this does not occur, revisit each aggregate and reaffirm them as sources of suffering. Relinquish them from all sides, focusing on the central point, and you will be led to the state of emptiness.

**Understanding Emptiness:**
In the state of emptiness, recognize that even this state is subject to change and can be a cause of stress. Understand that clinging to emptiness as self will lead to suffering when it changes. If you do not attain the initial stage of liberation, discern: "I relinquish the emptiness, I relinquish!" Recognize that even emptiness is a preparation of the mind and is subject to change. This realization helps you focus on a state beyond emptiness.

**Experiencing the State Beyond Emptiness:**
Strive to overcome the state of emptiness to reach a level beyond it. This process will help you experience the initial stage of liberation, which may last for a few seconds or minutes. With continued practice, you can maintain this state of liberation for longer periods. Ultimately, you will achieve a profound state of liberation where all preparations are stilled, experiencing deep and enduring peace. This state is free from the suffering inherent in all aggregates and offers a profound and lasting tranquillity.

Dukkha Anupassana:

# 26

# Anatta Anupassana:

## *Discerning Non-Self*

To begin this meditation, find a comfortable sitting position with your spine straight. Close your eyes gently, bringing your awareness inward. This practice, known as "Anatta Anupassana," or the discerning of non-self, will guide you to understand the nature of your body, sensations, perceptions, volitional activities, and consciousness as not truly belonging to you, not as yourself or a soul, but rather as phenomena that arise and pass away without any true ownership or control.

### 1. Discerning the Non-Self Nature of the Body

Start by reflecting on your body. Bring to mind various stages of your life—your childhood, your teenage years, your early adulthood. Recall specific moments, perhaps when you were five years old, then when you were fifteen, and then twenty. Notice how your body has changed over the years. Consider how, as a child, you couldn't choose the way your body would grow or develop. You couldn't dictate your height, your facial features, or your physical abilities. These changes happened independently of your wishes, and this lack of control over your body's transformation is a clear sign that the body is not truly "you." It is not yours to command or alter according to your desires.

Next, think about the future. Imagine your body as it might be in ten years, twenty years, or even when you are old. You may wish to remain youthful, healthy, and strong, but despite your desires, your body will continue to age, get sick, and eventually die. You cannot stop this process, just as you couldn't control your body's development in the past. This inevitability reinforces the understanding that your body is not under your control; it is not your true self.

Now, bring your attention to the present moment. Feel your body as it is right now, sitting in meditation. Can you make your body stay exactly as it is, without changing? You might wish for your body to always be comfortable, free from pain or discomfort, but you cannot prevent the natural sensations that arise—aches, itches, or the urge to move. This inability to control your body's experience in this very moment is another indication that the body is not "you." It is simply a collection of elements subject to change, decay, and eventual dissolution.

As you reflect on the body's impermanence and lack of control, deeply understand that the body is not you. It is not yours. It is not your self or soul. The body is merely a vessel, constantly changing, and ultimately, it does not belong to anyone.

## 2. Discerning the Non-Self Nature of Sensations

Next, turn your attention to sensations. Recall past experiences of sensation—perhaps the most intense pleasure you have ever felt, or the deepest pain. Notice how those sensations have come and gone, completely out of your control. You might have wanted a pleasurable sensation to last forever, but it faded away. Similarly, you might have wished for pain to end instantly, but it persisted until it naturally passed. This shows that sensations are not under your control—they arise and cease according to conditions, not according to your will.

Consider the future as well. Imagine future experiences that might bring you pleasure or pain. Even though you may want to hold on to pleasant sensations or avoid unpleasant ones, you cannot control their occurrence or duration. The sensations will arise and pass away just as they did in the past, further illustrating that they are not "you" or "yours."

Now, bring your awareness to the present sensations in your body. Perhaps you feel warmth, coolness, pressure, or a subtle vibration. Observe these sensations without attachment, recognizing that they are constantly changing and beyond your control. Just as in the past and future, the sensations you experience now are not you. They are not your self or soul; they are simply fleeting experiences that come and go.

### 3. Discerning the Non-Self Nature of Perceptions

Move your focus to perceptions. Recall past moments when you perceived something—perhaps the way you saw someone, a sound you heard, or a thought you believed to be true. Notice how your perceptions have shifted over time. What you once perceived as true or real may no longer seem so. This inconsistency reveals that perceptions are not stable, and they are not under your control. They change based on circumstances, experiences, and time.

Think about the future. Imagine how your perceptions might change—how you might see things differently as you grow older or as your experiences evolve. Just as in the past, your future perceptions will shift and change, independent of your desires. This reinforces the understanding that perceptions are not "you." They are not yours to hold on to or control.

In the present moment, observe your current perceptions. Notice how you perceive your surroundings, the sounds around you, or even your thoughts. Can you make your perceptions stay the same? Do you have control over how you perceive things right now? As you reflect on this, understand that perceptions are not your true self. They are temporary, ever-changing, and ultimately beyond your control.

4. **Discerning the Non-Self Nature of Volitional Activities**

Next, turn your attention to volitional activities, which include your thoughts, intentions, and decisions. Reflect on past decisions or thoughts that you had—how they arose and then disappeared. Notice how many of your thoughts and decisions were influenced by external factors, emotions, or circumstances beyond your control. You might have had thoughts that you wished to get rid of, or decisions that you later regretted. This shows that your volitional activities are not entirely yours to command.

Consider the future. Think about the decisions you will make, the thoughts you will have. Just as in the past, these future volitional activities will arise due to various causes and conditions, and they will not be under your absolute control. This understanding helps you see that these activities are not your true self.

Now, observe your present thoughts and intentions. Watch as they arise and pass away, often without your conscious effort. You may try to control your thoughts, but they continue to change. This lack of control indicates that volitional activities are not "you." They are not your self or soul; they are just processes happening on their own.

5. **Discerning the Non-Self Nature of Consciousness**

Finally, bring your focus to consciousness itself. Reflect on your past experiences of consciousness—how your awareness has shifted over time. Perhaps in the past, your consciousness was focused on a particular goal or desire, only for that focus to change as circumstances changed. This fluctuation shows that consciousness is not stable or under your control.

Think about the future. Consider how your consciousness will change as you age, as you experience different stages of life, and as your mind evolves. Just as with the body, sensations, perceptions, and volitional activities, your consciousness will also continue to change, independent of your desires. This further illustrates that consciousness is not your true self.

In the present moment, observe your consciousness. Notice how it shifts from one thought to another, from one experience to another. You cannot hold your consciousness in one state; it is constantly moving and changing. This ever-changing nature of consciousness reveals that it is not "you." It is not your self or soul, but simply a process that arises and passes away.

**Attaining Emptiness and Moving Beyond**

After deeply understanding the non-self nature of the body, sensations, perceptions, volitional activities, and consciousness in the past, future, and present, your mind may naturally settle into a state of emptiness. If this does not happen, quickly review the five aggregates again—body, sensations, perceptions, volitional activities, and consciousness—and relinquish them into five sides, concentrating on the center.

In this state of emptiness, recognize that even this state is impermanent. It, too, is not your true self. As you relinquish attachment to the emptiness, you move beyond it, attaining a state of profound liberation. This state is free from any perception of self, even beyond emptiness itself, leading to the stilling of all preparations and the experience of deep and enduring peace.

This ultimate liberation is the cessation of all suffering, where the mind rests in complete stillness, free from the clinging and grasping that causes distress. This state, especially when attained in the fourth stage of complete liberation, offers profound and lasting tranquility, surpassing even the state of emptiness, and leading to the ultimate peace that is beyond all suffering and stress.

# 27
# Nirodha Anupassana:
## *Discerning the Cessation of All Phenomena*

The meditation on cessation, known as "Nirodha Anupassana," invites you to observe the end of phenomena rather than their arising or constant change. While impermanence (Anicca) involves noticing how things continuously arise and pass away, cessation (Nirodha) focuses purely on the passing away, the cessation, of things without the distraction of their beginnings or middles. This approach is a profound and subtle form of insight, leading to a deep understanding of the nature of existence and the path to ultimate liberation, Nibbana.

**Understanding Cessation Through the Experience of Breath**

In this practice, we will use the breath, a constant and ever-present experience, as our primary object of meditation. The breath serves as an excellent tool to discern the cessation of phenomena because it is both tangible and subtle, and it occurs naturally without any need for interference or control.

1. **Focusing on the Cessation of the Breath**

   Begin by settling into a comfortable sitting position with your spine straight and your body relaxed. Close your eyes gently and bring your awareness to the breath. Rather than focusing on the entire process of breathing, direct your attention specifically to the cessation of each breath. Notice how the breath in comes to an end before the breath out begins. Then, observe how the breath out ceases before the next breath in starts. Spend several minutes simply watching this cycle of cessation: the ending of the inhalation and the ending of the exhalation. Allow your mind to rest in the awareness of the breath's cessation, observing how each moment of breathing passes away, never to return.

2. **Observing the Cessation of Sensations**

   After you have spent some time with the breath itself, shift your focus to the sensations associated with the breath. Notice the subtle sensations that arise as the breath enters and leaves your nostrils, perhaps a coolness or warmth. Now, instead of dwelling on the arising of these sensations, concentrate on their cessation. Watch how the sensation of coolness disappears as the breath moves inward, and how the warmth fades as the breath exits. Observe how each sensation, subtle or pronounced, ceases as the breath flows in and out. This cessation of sensations with each breath underscores the transient nature of all experiences, helping you to discern that sensations are not enduring, not stable, and therefore not truly self.

3. **Discerning the Cessation of Perceptions**

   As you continue to observe the breath, bring your attention to the perceptions that arise with each breath. Every time you breathe in, there is a subtle perception: "I am breathing in." With each breath out, there is a perception: "I am breathing out." Focus on the moment when these perceptions end. Notice how, at the end of the inhalation, the perception of "breathing in" ceases, and at the end of the exhalation, the perception of "breathing out" fades away. Spend several minutes observing this, recognizing that even your perceptions, which seem so immediate and intimate, are subject to cessation. They arise and pass without any true substance or permanence.

4. **Cessation of Consciousness**

   As you deepen your focus, notice that during the cycle of breathing in and out, and the sensations and perceptions associated with it, there is a reduction in volitional activities—the intentional actions of the mind. When you simply observe without interference, the mind naturally begins to settle, and the usual cycle of mental activities begins to cease. In this stillness, volitional activities become increasingly subtle, at this point, discern the cessation of consciousness itself—the awareness of the breath. As you breathe in and out, consciousness arises with each breath, but it also ceases. Focus on this cessation, noticing how consciousness associated with the breath ends each time, reinforcing the understanding that even consciousness is not self; it too arises and passes according to conditions.

**Going Deeper: The Micro-Cessation of Breath, Sensations, Perceptions, and Consciousness**

Now, take your practice deeper by breaking down the breath into finer segments. Observe the cessation not just at the end of each breath, but within each breath itself. Notice how the beginning of the breath in ceases as it reaches the middle, and how the middle ceases as it reaches the end. The same applies to the breath out—each segment of the breath arises and ceases in quick succession. This micro-analysis of the breath allows you to see the cessation at every moment, helping you to realize that the breath is not a continuous, unbroken experience but a series of momentary cessations.

Apply this same scrutiny to the sensations, perceptions, and consciousness. As the breath flows in, break down the sensation into its beginning, middle, and end, observing how each part ceases before the next begins. Do the same with perceptions—observe how the perception of the breath in ceases before the next perception arises. Finally, observe consciousness in this way, noticing how it flickers in and out of existence with each breath.

**Attaining Emptiness and Going Beyond**

As you continue to focus on the constant fast cessation of breath, sensations, perceptions, and consciousness, faster than discerning start-middle-end, you may reach a point where your mind spontaneously slips into a state of emptiness. This is a natural progression, as the continuous observation of cessation leads to the fading away of mental activities and the arising of emptiness. However, this state of emptiness is not the end goal; it is another phenomenon subject to cessation.

To go beyond this stage, watch the cessation of even this empty consciousness. Recognize that emptiness itself is impermanent, a passing state that is not your true self. As you relinquish attachment to this state, you may glimpse Nibbana, the ultimate cessation—free from all formations, empty of all phenomena, and utterly peaceful.

In this practice of Nirodha Anupassana, you move beyond the surface of things, beyond the arising and passing of phenomena, to the profound realization of cessation. By discerning cessation at every level—breath, sensation, perception, volitional activity, and consciousness—you gain insight into the true nature of reality. This insight leads to the stilling of all preparations, the cessation of all clinging, and the direct experience of Nibbana, the supreme peace that lies beyond the cycle of birth, suffering, and death.

This practice is not merely an intellectual exercise but a deep, transformative meditation that can lead to profound liberation. By repeatedly observing the cessation of phenomena, you weaken the attachment to the illusion of self, leading to the gradual unfolding of wisdom and the ultimate realization of the deathless, Nibbana.

# 28
# Patinissagga Anupassana:
## *Discerning the Relinquishment of All Attachments*

In the practice of "Patinissagga Anupassana," we focus on the relinquishment of all desires and attachments, understanding that these are the sources of stress and suffering. This meditation is a profound exercise in letting go—of people, possessions, ideas, and even the very process of letting go itself. By relinquishing attachment to all phenomena, we liberate the mind from the burdens that cause suffering and move toward the stilling of all mental activities, ultimately leading to the supreme peace of Nibbana.

**The Body: An Enemy in Disguise**

Begin this meditation by adopting a straight spine, sitting comfortably yet alert. Close your eyes and turn your attention inward, beginning with the body. Reflect on the true nature of the body, not as a friend or ally but as an enemy that constantly seeks to betray you. This body is a source of endless trouble—it falls ill, ages, decays, and ultimately dies. It is a fragile vessel, subject to disease, pain, and discomfort, and no matter how much we care for it, it is destined to deteriorate.

Consider how the body deceives you with its temporary pleasures, leading you to believe in its worth and solidity. But in truth, it is nothing more than a collection of impermanent elements, always in flux, never truly under your control. The body, with its endless needs and vulnerabilities, is a cause of suffering. It binds you to the cycle of birth, aging, illness, and death. As you meditate on this reality, allow a sense of disgust to arise—a clear understanding that this body is not something to cherish or cling to. It is a source of stress, not satisfaction.

To aid in this reflection, silently repeat to yourself: "I relinquish! I relinquish the body." With each repetition, feel the attachment to the body loosening. Imagine yourself unshackling from this heavy burden, letting go of the false belief that the body is truly yours or that it can bring lasting happiness.

**Sensations: Deceptive and Fleeting**

Next, turn your attention to the sensations that arise in the body. These sensations—whether pleasant, unpleasant, or neutral—are fleeting and deceptive. They are conditioned responses to stimuli, constantly arising and passing away, offering no true satisfaction.

Consider how much of your life is spent chasing pleasant sensations and avoiding unpleasant ones, only to find that neither brings lasting peace. Pleasant sensations quickly fade, leaving behind a craving for more. Unpleasant sensations bring discomfort and aversion, leading to mental agitation. Even neutral sensations, though subtle, can lead to boredom and restlessness.

Reflect on how these sensations, like the body itself, are sources of stress. They arise without your control and vanish just as quickly, offering no stability or refuge. As you meditate on this, allow a sense of dispassion to develop—a recognition that clinging to sensations only perpetuates the cycle of suffering.

To help relinquish this attachment, silently repeat: "I relinquish! I relinquish the sensations." As you do so, feel the grip of these fleeting experiences loosen, and allow your mind to settle into a deeper state of equanimity, free from the constant pursuit of sensory pleasure or the avoidance of pain.

**Perceptions: The Illusion of Meaning**

Now, direct your attention to perceptions—the mental labels and interpretations that your mind applies to the world around you. Perceptions create the illusion of meaning and identity, causing you to believe that things are good or bad, desirable or undesirable. But like sensations, perceptions are impermanent and unreliable. They are conditioned by past experiences and cultural conditioning, often leading you to cling to ideas and concepts that only reinforce suffering.

Consider how perceptions can trap you in cycles of craving and aversion. For example, perceiving something as beautiful can lead to attachment and desire, while perceiving something as ugly can lead to aversion and rejection. Both responses are rooted in ignorance, as they fail to see the true nature of phenomena as impermanent and not-self.

As you meditate on the impermanence and unreliability of perceptions, allow a sense of detachment to arise. Recognize that perceptions, like sensations, are not worth clinging to. They do not represent ultimate truth but are merely mental constructs that arise and pass away.

Silently repeat: "I relinquish! I relinquish the perceptions." With each repetition, feel your attachment to perceptions diminish. Allow your mind to become more spacious, free from the constricting influence of mental labels and judgments.

**Relinquishing All Attachments**

Having relinquished attachment to the body, sensations, and perceptions, extend this practice to all other areas of life. Relinquish your attachment to people—your children, parents, spouse, loved ones. Reflect on how these relationships, while meaningful, are also sources of stress and potential suffering. They are subject to change, and clinging to them only leads to heartache.

Next, relinquish your attachment to material possessions—your home, vehicle, profession, job, properties, and bank account. Recognize that these things, no matter how valuable they seem, are impermanent and ultimately beyond your control. They can be lost, stolen, or destroyed, and the more you cling to them, the more you set yourself up for suffering.

Go further still and relinquish your attachment to ideas and beliefs—the desire for living, the desire for death, the ideas of good and bad, even your devotion to the Lord Buddha, Dhamma, and Sangha. Understand that while these concepts may guide you on your path, they are still mental formations, subject to change and impermanence.

Finally, relinquish all spiritual aspirations, including the desire for spiritual growth, equanimity, and even the desire for Nibbana itself. Recognize that clinging to these goals can also be a source of stress, as it creates a sense of striving and a sense of self that must achieve something.

Silently repeat: "I relinquish! I relinquish all attachments." As you do so, feel yourself letting go of every clinging thought, desire, and attachment. Imagine yourself as a bird soaring high above, free from the weight of worldly concerns, free from the chains of craving and attachment.

**Relinquishing the Concept of Relinquishment**

Having relinquished everything else, even relinquish the concept of relinquishment. Recognize that the idea of letting go itself can become an attachment if clung to too tightly. True liberation comes not from the act of letting go but from the understanding that there is nothing to cling to in the first place.

At this point, the mind may naturally enter a state of emptiness, free from all mental formations. However, even this state of emptiness is not the end goal. It, too, is impermanent and subject to change. As you become aware of this, discern the consciousness of the empty state as another source of stress.

Relinquish attachment to this empty consciousness, understanding that it is also not your true self. As you let go of even the awareness of emptiness, you move toward the ultimate stilling of all preparations—the cessation of all mental activities, where true peace and liberation lie.

**The Stilling of All Preparations: The Path to Nibbana**

In this practice of Patinissagga Anupassana, you systematically relinquish every attachment, from the grossest physical forms to the subtlest mental concepts. By doing so, you free the mind from the causes of suffering and move closer to the stilling of all preparations, the ultimate state of equanimity and peace.

This stilling is not a state of emptiness or void but a profound liberation from all that binds you to the cycle of birth and death. It is the realization of Nibbana, where there is no more clinging, no more craving, no more suffering—only the pure, unconditioned peace of liberation.

Through this meditation, you cultivate the wisdom to see all phenomena as impermanent, stressful, and not-self. You develop the detachment necessary to relinquish all that causes suffering, and in doing so, you move closer to the ultimate goal of the Buddhist path: the attainment of Nibbana, the cessation of all suffering, and the realization of the deathless state.

# 29
# Awareness Meditation:
## *A Path to Stilling the Mind and Attaining Liberation*

In this chapter, we explore an advanced form of meditation that can be practiced with eyes open, cultivating a heightened awareness of sensory experiences while moving toward the ultimate goal of stilling the mind. This meditation requires a firm comprehension of the concept of non-self (anatta), a foundational teaching in the Buddha's Dhamma. By deeply understanding that everything we perceive—whether visual, auditory, or physical—is impermanent and not a true "self," we can disengage from attachment and dissolve the illusion of individuality.

**Preparing the Mind: Understanding Non-Self**

Before engaging in this meditation, it's crucial to reflect on the concept of non-self. All phenomena, whether external objects or internal thoughts and sensations, are subject to change. They are impermanent (anicca), and therefore, they are not worth clinging to. This understanding allows the meditator to adopt a detached, equanimous attitude toward all sensory experiences.

Imagine looking at a river. It constantly flows, and no drop of water remains still. Similarly, the sights you see, the sounds you hear, and the sensations you feel are constantly shifting, fleeting, and beyond your control. Just as you cannot hold onto a single drop of water from a rushing stream, you cannot grasp any of the passing sensory experiences. Recognizing this fundamental truth is the foundation for deepening awareness and moving toward relinquishment of attachment.

**Entering the Meditation: Engaging the Senses with Awareness**

Begin by sitting with your spine straight. This upright posture is a symbol of alertness and readiness to engage fully in the practice. The meditation starts with your eyes open, but the goal is not to focus on any particular object. Rather, it is to maintain a broad, diffuse awareness of the entire visual field. Think of it as seeing everything and nothing simultaneously.

1. **Visual Awareness:** Start by directing your attention to your overall field of vision. You are not focusing on any one object or detail; instead, you are aware of the entirety of what is before your eyes. The mind often wants to name or categorize things—"this is a

tree," "that is a car"—but in this practice, you simply observe without labeling or judging. Allow the visual field to be exactly as it is, acknowledging it but not attaching to any particular aspect of it.

2. **Auditory Awareness:** Once you feel settled in your visual awareness, move to sound. Focus on the overall experience of hearing without zeroing in on any specific sound. Whether it's the distant hum of a fan, the chirping of birds, or the rustle of leaves, let your mind become a passive observer of all auditory sensations. Avoid identifying the sources of the sounds or attaching any significance to them. Simply acknowledge the experience of hearing itself.
3. **Tactile Awareness:** Next, bring your attention to the sense of touch. This includes all bodily sensations—temperature, the feeling of your clothes on your skin, or the contact between your body and the chair. Like with visual and auditory awareness, you do not need to focus on any one sensation. Instead, you cultivate a broad awareness of all tangible experiences without attempting to name or categorize them.

### Maintaining Mindful Awareness: Overcoming Thought Intrusion

During this process, thoughts may arise in the mind. Thoughts are the natural outcome of sensory inputs and habitual patterns of the mind. However, in this meditation, the key is to not let the thoughts take over or grow into full mental narratives. The moment a thought arises—whether it's about the past, future, or something in the present—shift your attention immediately to one of the three sensory doors: vision, sound, or touch.

For example, if a thought about work comes up, instead of engaging with it, immediately shift your attention back to the soundscape. This quick shift helps prevent the mind from getting entangled in thoughts, allowing you to remain present and aware.

By practicing this repeatedly, the mind becomes accustomed to not getting stuck in its own stories. It learns to navigate the space between thoughts, allowing awareness to become more fluid and spacious.

**Speeding Up the Process: Developing Full Awareness**

As you become more proficient in this practice, you can gradually speed up the process. Instead of spending several moments on each sense, move from one sense to the next more quickly—every second or so. The goal is to cultivate simultaneous awareness of all three sensory domains: vision, sound, and touch.

This simultaneous awareness creates a state of complete mindfulness, where the mind is fully engaged with the present moment and the external world without being distracted by internal commentary. It's like balancing on a tightrope—if you hesitate or lean too far in one direction, you lose your balance. But by maintaining awareness of all three senses without clinging to any particular one, you create a powerful state of mental stillness.

In this state, you become "stuck in the awareness," but in a positive sense—completely absorbed in the present moment without the interference of thoughts or perceptions. The mind becomes deeply peaceful, as it is no longer caught up in the habitual cycles of craving, aversion, and identification.

**Transitioning to Eyes Closed: Stilling of Preparations**

After a time, you may naturally feel inclined to close your eyes. When this happens, follow the urge and allow your eyes to gently close. With the eyes closed, your awareness shifts inward. You have already developed a heightened sense of awareness through the open-eyed practice, and now, with eyes closed, the mind begins to settle into a deeper state of stillness.

At this stage, you may experience subtle thoughts or perceptions about the "empty state" of the mind. These can include feelings of peace or clarity, or perhaps a sense of spaciousness or emptiness. However, it is important not to cling even to these refined states. While they may feel peaceful, they too are impermanent and not-self.

Discern that even the subtle perception of emptiness is still subject to change. It, too, will arise and pass away, just like all other phenomena. Therefore, relinquish any attachment to this state. Recognize it as impermanent, and mentally repeat: "This too is not myself." By doing so, you let go of the last vestiges of attachment, bringing the mind to an even deeper state of quietude.

**The Final Stage: Relinquishing Even Awareness Itself**

As you progress in this meditation, you will reach a point where the mind no longer clings to any sensory experience, thought, or perception. At this point, the stilling of all preparations occurs. This is the cessation of all mental activities, where the mind enters a state of profound stillness.

But even here, you must remain vigilant. Awareness itself can become a subtle object of attachment. If there is still the perception of being aware, recognize that this awareness, too, is impermanent and not-self.

Once you relinquish even the awareness of awareness, the mind transcends all conditioned states. This is the doorway to Nibbana, the unconditioned, where all suffering ceases, and there is no longer any identification with body, mind, or self.

**Conclusion: The Path to Nibbana Through Awareness Meditation**

This awareness meditation, when practiced diligently, can bring the mind to a state of complete stillness, where all mental formations cease, and the illusion of self is fully relinquished. By paying close attention to the sensory world without attaching to it, you gradually dissolve the mental habits that cause suffering.

The key to success in this practice is understanding the impermanent and non-self nature of all phenomena. Whether it is the body, sounds, sensations, thoughts, or even awareness itself, nothing is truly "you." By relinquishing everything, you reach the ultimate peace that lies beyond all attachment—the stilling of all preparations and the realization of Nibbana.

Through this practice, you train the mind to remain in the present moment without clinging or grasping. And in doing so, you lay the foundation for the highest liberation, freeing yourself from the cycle of suffering and attaining the supreme goal of life: Nibbana.

# 30
# Duality Meditation:
## *Transcending the Illusion of Separation to Attain Nibbāna*

In this chapter, we delve into a profound meditation practice designed to reveal the illusion of duality and ultimately lead to the realization of Nibbāna. This meditation hinges on the understanding that the perception of a separate "world" and "self" is an illusion—an outcome of ignorance (avijjā) and mental conditioning. By discerning the mind's tendency to show duality, the meditator can cut through this illusion and experience reality as it truly is, without the false division of "self" and "other."

**The Nature of Duality: A Mechanism of Ignorance**

To comprehend this meditation, it is essential to recognize that duality—our perception of "me" and the "world"—is a product of mental constructions. In reality, there is only consciousness arising and passing away from moment to moment. However, the mind, conditioned by ignorance, distorts these basic experiences by presenting a false dichotomy: a separate self (the observer) and an external world (the observed).

Let's take the example of hearing a bird chirping. Initially, there is the bare experience of sound—this is the arising of auditory consciousness. But the mind, programmed to perpetuate the illusion of self, immediately follows this with a division: "I am hearing the bird" and "the bird exists independently of me." This sense of duality is not inherent in the experience of consciousness itself but is a mental creation layered on top of it. The moment the consciousness arises, the mind interprets and projects the idea of a bird and an observer (me) as independently existing entities. This mental division is the root of suffering and delusion.

However, when examined closely, it becomes clear that the bird, the sound, and the "I" who hears it are all mere constructions of the mind. They arise from the same consciousness and are part of the same process. The division is an illusion—one that can be transcended through mindful observation.

**Step 1: Establishing Awareness of the Breath**

To begin this meditation, sit with your spine straight and close your eyes. Bring your attention to the natural flow of the breath. Focus on the point where the breath touches—either just inside or outside the nostrils. This is the tangible, direct experience that will serve as the anchor for your awareness.

As you breathe in and out, observe this point of contact. This initial step is about developing a keen, moment-to-moment awareness of the breath without adding any judgments or interpretations. You are simply aware of the sensation where the breath meets the nostrils.

**Step 2: Observing the Duality in the Breath**

Now, pay attention to how the mind automatically divides the experience of breathing into two distinct components: the air (the external element) and the nose (the internal element). For example, as you breathe in, the mind may say, "Here is the air entering, and here is my nose feeling the air." This is the mind creating duality.

Similarly, if you were to touch your leg to the floor, the mind immediately conceives, "Here is the floor, and here is my leg." The same pattern arises with the breath: "Here is the air, and here is my nose." This division is automatic, but it is not an inherent part of the experience—it is simply a mental construction, a habit of the mind.

In reality, there is no such inherent separation between the air and the nose, the observer and the observed. They are part of a single, unified process. However, due to ignorance, the mind continually conceives them as two independent entities.

**Step 3: Discerning Thoughtful Duality**

Once you have identified this duality, the next step is to observe it with understanding. Recognize that this division—air and nose, observer and observed—is merely a thought arising in the mind. It is not a reality; it is a mental fabrication. This is what we call "thoughtful duality" because it is a product of thought, not a reflection of true reality.

You might discern the duality in this way: “This is thoughtful air, and this is thoughtful nose.” You are not denying that you experience air or that you experience the sensation of the nose, but you are acknowledging that the division between them is a construction of the mind.

Continue to observe the breath with this understanding. Each time the mind presents the duality of air and nose, recognize it as merely a thought. Over time, you will see that this duality becomes less convincing. The mind begins to recognize that it has been creating an illusion. When the illusion is exposed, it loses its power.

**Step 4: Letting Go of Duality**

As you continue to practice, something profound will happen: the mind will stop presenting the duality. Once you see through the illusion, it can no longer hold sway over you. When duality ceases to arise, you are left with pure awareness. You are simply aware of the breath, without the division between air and nose, self and other, observer and observed.

In this state of pure awareness, the mind is no longer divided. It experiences reality as it truly is—a seamless, unified process, without the artificial distinctions created by ignorance. The breath is just the breath. There is no "me" who breathes and no "air" that is separate from the breath. There is only the direct experience of breathing.

This is a powerful state of mental clarity and calm. With sustained practice, you will naturally feel drawn into deeper levels of concentration. You may find yourself entering a state of emptiness or profound stillness. At this point, you may choose to allow yourself to sink further into this state.

**Step 5: Insight into Emptiness and the Self**

As you rest in this state of emptiness, another layer of duality may appear: the sense of a "self" experiencing emptiness. Just as before, the mind may create a division between the emptiness (the observed) and the "I" who experiences it (the observer). This is yet another layer of illusion.

Recognize this duality as well. Understand that the sense of "self" and the emptiness are both products of thought. There is no independent "self" experiencing emptiness. There is only the experience of emptiness itself, arising and passing in consciousness.

Discern this emptiness as impermanent and non-self, just as you did with the breath. With this insight, you can relinquish even the attachment to emptiness and the sense of "I." When this final duality is let go of, the mind is liberated. It is no longer bound by the illusion of self or other, subject or object. It rests in the unconditioned state of Nibbāna.

**Applying Duality Meditation in Daily Life**

This meditation is not limited to formal sitting practice. It can be applied in everyday situations. For example, when someone scolds you, the mind immediately creates a duality: "Here is the person who scolded me" and "Here is me, the one who was scolded." This division leads to feelings of anger, hurt, or resentment. However, if you apply the principles of duality meditation, you can see that the scolding and the "self" who was scolded are both constructions of the mind. They are just thoughts, arising and passing like any other.

Similarly, when lust arises after seeing someone attractive, the mind creates the division between "the attractive person" and "me, the one who desires." But by practicing this meditation, you can observe that the lust and the sense of self are merely thoughts. Once you see through the illusion, the craving diminishes.

**Conclusion: The Path to Liberation through Duality Meditation**

Through this practice of duality meditation, the mind systematically deconstructs the illusions that bind it to suffering. By discerning the duality in every experience—whether it be the breath, the sense of self, or the world around you—you gradually see through the layers of ignorance and mental constructions that perpetuate suffering.

Like a robot programmed to interpret sensory data, the mind has been conditioned to divide reality into "me" and "the world." But when we closely examine this mechanism, we realize that this division is an illusion. It is not a reflection of how things truly are; it is a mental fabrication.

As the mind learns to let go of this duality, it enters into a state of pure awareness—undivided, peaceful, and free from conceptual overlay. Eventually, the mind transcends even this state, realizing the ultimate truth of Nibbāna, the cessation of suffering and the end of ignorance.

By practicing duality meditation, you take a direct step toward liberation, breaking the chains of delusion and discovering the true nature of reality. This path leads to the cessation of all dualities, all divisions, and ultimately, the complete freedom from suffering.

# 31
# Walking Meditation:
## *A Path to Liberation through Awareness of Duality and Beyond*

Walking meditation, a time-honored practice in many spiritual traditions, offers a unique opportunity to cultivate mindfulness and insight, even in motion. Unlike seated meditation, where the body remains still, walking meditation allows us to explore awareness in a dynamic way, synchronizing our physical movement with mental clarity. This chapter explores how walking meditation can be a powerful tool for insight into the nature of duality, and how it leads us to pure awareness, emptiness, and ultimately, liberation.

### Preparation for Walking Meditation

Before beginning the practice, choose a straight, flat path that is at least 30 feet long. This will allow you to walk back and forth without distraction or obstacles. Walking slowly and mindfully, we will apply the principles of duality meditation—discerning the nature of the mind's tendency to divide experiences into dualistic concepts like "me" and "the world"—to our walking.

**Step 1: Observing the Tangible Feeling**

Begin by simply walking and focusing on the sensations in your feet as they touch the ground. Feel the texture, the temperature, and the pressure of the ground beneath you. As you walk, refrain from engaging in any thought other than being fully aware of the tangible feel of your feet.

At this stage, you are grounding yourself in direct sensory experience, much like the way you start focusing on the breath in seated meditation. This initial focus on the foot's touch is essential for anchoring awareness in the present moment and quieting the mind.

**Step 2: Recognizing the Duality of Experience**

As you continue to walk, you'll naturally begin to notice how your mind creates a sense of division between your feet and the ground. Your mind will say, "Here is the floor, and here is my foot." This is the experience of duality—the notion that there is a "me" who is walking and an "external world" beneath the feet.

Observe how your mind automatically divides the experience into two distinct parts: the floor and the foot. At this moment, the duality becomes apparent: "I" am the one walking on the "floor." This is a crucial step in walking meditation, as it helps you see how the mind constructs the illusion of separation.

For example, if you were to touch your leg on the floor while sitting, your mind would tell you, "Here is the leg, and here is the floor," dividing the single experience of contact into two entities. Similarly, while walking, the mind creates the illusion of "I" and "the floor." By becoming aware of this process, you begin to see how duality is fabricated by the mind.

**Step 3: Understanding Duality as a Thought**

Once you've discerned the duality, take a step further by recognizing that this division is not inherent in reality—it is a product of thought. The "floor" and "foot" exist as separate entities only because the mind perceives them that way. In truth, the moment of experience is simply the tangible sensation of foot and ground meeting, and any interpretation of "floor" or "foot" is a mental construction.

Watch how the mind labels these experiences and divides them into subject and object, observer and observed. With practice, you'll begin to see that this duality is merely a thought—a conceptual layer added to the raw experience of walking. There is no "independent" floor or "independent" foot outside of the mind's projection.

**Step 4: Walking with Pure Awareness**

As you continue walking, you will notice that once you understand duality as a product of thought, the mind will naturally stop creating it. There will come a point when duality disappears, and all that remains is the pure awareness of walking. At this stage, you are no longer thinking of "my foot" or "the floor"; you are simply walking, fully absorbed in the present moment, without the interference of conceptualization.

This experience of pure awareness is a powerful gateway to deeper concentration. With no mental division, you are walking with full mindfulness, free from the illusion of separation. The simplicity of this practice reveals the mind's natural capacity to be aware without distortion.

**Step 5: Entering Emptiness**

As you walk in this state of pure awareness, you may feel a growing desire to close your eyes and stand still. When this happens, allow yourself to stop and stand upright. Close your eyes and enter into the emptiness that arises.

This emptiness is not a void but a profound sense of spaciousness where the mind is no longer divided. It is an experience of being beyond duality, where thoughts of "me" and "the world" dissolve. Yet even here, recognize that this experience of emptiness itself can be another subtle form of duality. The mind might still conceive of "me" experiencing the "emptiness."

**Step 6: Insight into Emptiness**

At this point, insight becomes crucial. Just as we discern duality as a thought, we now discern that emptiness is also a form of duality—a subtle, refined concept created by the mind. By understanding that this emptiness is impermanent and non-self, you can relinquish attachment to it.

The final step in this meditation is to see even emptiness as a mental fabrication and go beyond it. In this relinquishing, the mind transcends both duality and emptiness, entering into the realm of liberation—Nibbāna. The cessation of all conceptualization, even of "emptiness" or "self," leads to the ultimate freedom from suffering.

**Discerning of Cessation (Nirodha Anupassana) in Walking Meditation**

Another powerful technique you can apply during walking meditation is the practice of cessation (nirodha anupassana). This method involves closely observing the cessation of various mental and physical phenomena. Begin by watching the cessation of the tangible sensation in your feet after each step.

Then, expand your awareness to notice the cessation of sensations that arise while walking, such as the feeling of the ground or the movement of your legs. Next, observe the cessation of perception, the mind's interpretation of those sensations. Finally, watch the cessation of consciousness itself—the moment when your awareness of the step ends.

Once you feel a natural stopping point, stand still and close your eyes, entering into the emptiness once more. Use this insight to go beyond emptiness by discerning its impermanence and non-self nature, moving towards full liberation.

**Simpler Techniques: Observing the Legs and Posture**

For those new to walking meditation, a simpler version of this practice involves merely observing the movement of your legs as you walk. Focus on each part of the walking motion: lifting, moving, and placing the foot. Alternatively, you can practice by observing your entire body's posture as you walk, remaining mindful of the way your body moves through space.

These simpler practices can still lead to deep mindfulness, helping you develop a sense of presence and connection to the current moment, even if you don't yet explore duality in detail.

**Applying Walking Meditation in Daily Life**

Walking meditation is not limited to a formal practice session. You can apply the principles of this meditation to your daily life. Whether you are walking to work, taking a stroll in nature, or moving around your home, you can practice mindfulness of the body's movement, observing how the mind creates duality and how it can also relinquish it.

For instance, when you walk into a room, notice how the mind divides "me" and "the room," and then watch how that duality is just a thought. By integrating walking meditation into your everyday activities, you can deepen your mindfulness and insight into the nature of reality.

**Conclusion: Walking the Path to Liberation**

Walking meditation, like all forms of mindfulness, is a practice that helps us cultivate clarity and insight into the nature of our mind. By discerning the duality inherent in our perceptions and understanding that it is merely a product of thought, we can experience pure awareness and go beyond the illusion of separation. Eventually, through the practice of cessation and insight into emptiness, we can walk the path to Nibbāna—liberation from suffering.

# 32
# Brahma Vihara and Samatha Meditation:
## *The Path to Higher Concentration*

Samatha meditation, also known as tranquilizing meditation, is a practice taught by Lord Buddha that leads the mind into deep tranquility and concentration. Among the 40 Samatha meditation techniques, four of them are particularly revered, called the **Brahma Vihara**. The term "Brahma Vihara" translates to "dwelling place of Brahmas." Brahmas are celestial beings who reside in higher realms, and their qualities include **unlimited goodwill**, **unlimited compassion**, **unlimited empathetic joy**, and **unlimited equanimity**.

Lord Buddha proclaimed that by cultivating these four divine qualities—loving-kindness (Metta), compassion (Karuna), empathetic joy (Mudita), and equanimity (Upekkha)—one can tranquilize the mind to the point of attaining high levels of concentration, also known as **jhanas**, which lead to profound states of bliss and peace. These meditations are outlined in several Suttas, but particularly in the **Mettāsahagata Sutta**, which describes how these qualities can lead to deep concentration and even liberation.

## 1. Loving-kindness (Metta) Meditation

### Introduction to Metta

Metta meditation is the practice of cultivating and radiating **unconditional loving-kindness** toward oneself and others. It begins with focusing on one specific individual, usually a spiritual friend or respected teacher (but not a family member to avoid attachment). The practice then expands to encompass all beings in every direction of the universe.

### Instructions for Metta Meditation

- **Step 1: Selecting a person**

  Start by sitting with a straight spine and closing your eyes. Visualize the face of your spiritual friend or teacher, someone for whom you already have a natural sense of goodwill. Imagine their face clearly in your mind.

- **Step 2: Radiating loving-kindness**

From your heart, begin radiating Metta toward this person. Use the phrase: *"May he/she be free from hostility, free from affliction, free from distress; may he/she live happily."* After a few minutes, you can simplify this to the phrase: *"May he/she be happy!"* If it is hard to get the feeling of Metta, you can take recall a baby's smiling face and can get a smile to your face. This practice will help you to maintain loving-kindness while meditating.

- **Step 3: Feeling and radiating Metta**

The act of radiating Metta has two components. First, you **generate** the feeling of loving-kindness in your heart, and then, before the end of the phrase, you **radiate** that feeling toward the imagined face of your chosen person. This phase is essential as it combines both verbal and emotional components.

- **Step 4: Deepening the meditation**

After some time, you may feel he/she is smiling with you and may find that generating thoughts with the phrase becomes challenging. At this point, stop mentally chanting the phrase and focus solely on **radiating the feeling** of loving-kindness. When it becomes hard to radiate even the feeling, your mind will naturally begin to absorb into a deeper, concentrated state. Allow this absorption to happen and stay in this state as long as you can.

- **Step 5: Absorption and continuity**

If your concentration wavers, you can go back to the phrase and repeat the cycle: phrase → feeling → absorption. You may practice this for gradually increasing periods—15 minutes, 30 minutes, 45 minutes, up to an hour.

**Expanding Metta to Other Individuals and Directions**

- **Practice with different people**

Once you've developed strong Metta for your spiritual friend, move on to radiating loving-kindness toward a **loved one**, a **neutral person**, and finally an **antipathetic person**. Try to equalize the intensity of your loving-kindness for the antipathetic person with that of the loved one. This balances the mind and removes personal biases.

- **Radiating Metta in all directions**

After practicing with individuals, you can expand the meditation by radiating Metta to all beings in all directions: front, back, right, left, above, and below. Begin by using the phrase "May all beings be happy!" and focus on spreading loving-kindness as an **immeasurable** and **unlimited** force. After using the phrase for a while, switch to just the feeling of loving-kindness and absorb into it. Practice this up to two hours.

- **Ultimate concentration (Jhana)**

  Continue radiating Metta until you can cover the entire universe. Through this practice, you will begin to attain higher states of concentration, this leads to a profound state called **Subha Vimokkha** (the Liberation of Beauty).

**Liberation of Beauty (Subha Vimokkha)**

- **Perception transformation**

  After emerging from the absorption, contemplate something repulsive, such as excrement, and train the mind to perceive it as beautiful. Likewise, contemplate something beautiful, like a rose, and try to see it as repulsive. Then imagine both, and try to perceive both as similarly repulsive. Again, contemplate both, and try to perceive both as similarly beautiful. By alternating between these perceptions, you will understand that beauty and repulsiveness are merely **mental fabrications**. When this realization dawns, return to Metta and enter absorption. The mind will be clear and concentrated, leading to the state known as **Subha**

**Vimokkha**, the liberation through beauty perception. Practice this at least as a one hour absorption.

## 2. Compassion (Karuna) Meditation

### Transition from Metta to Karuna

After mastering Metta, the feeling of loving-kindness may start to feel subdued, and a quieter, more tranquil stage emerges. This is the transition to **compassion** (Karuna), which is a deep and subtle sense of wishing that all beings be free from suffering.

- **Radiating Compassion**

  Begin by radiating the feeling of compassion toward all beings, starting in the front direction and expanding to the other five directions. If the feeling of compassion is hard to generate, use the phrase:*"May all beings be free from suffering!"*

- **Absorption into Karuna**

  As with Metta, practice radiating the phrase until it becomes difficult, then move to just radiating the feeling of compassion. As you deepen this practice, you will eventually absorb into the state of **Karuna jhana**, which brings profound peace.

- **Attaining the Sphere of Infinite Space**

  According to the Mettāsahagata Sutta, the final outcome of Karuna meditation is the attainment of the **sphere of the infinitude of space**. After radiating compassion for two hours and mastering the feeling, direct your attention to the **infinity of space** that your compassion fills. By perceiving this **infinite space**, you will enter the **first formless jhana** (arupa jhana). Practice this stage gradually, extending it over multiple attempts up to two hours.

### 3. Empathetic Joy (Mudita) Meditation

#### Transition from Karuna to Mudita

Once Karuna is mastered, it begins to fade into a more subtle and joyful state. This transition marks the shift to **empathetic joy** (Mudita). Mudita is the feeling of rejoicing in the happiness and success of others.

- **Radiating Empathetic Joy**

  Begin by radiating Mudita toward all beings in each direction. If the feeling is hard to find, use the phrase:
  *"May all beings fulfil with joy!"*

- **Absorption into Mudita**

As you progress, the verbal phrases will become unnecessary, and the feeling of Mudita will naturally arise and radiate in all directions. Continue practicing until you reach the point of absorption.

- **Attaining the Sphere of Infinite Consciousness**

According to the Mettāsahagata Sutta, Mudita meditation culminates in the **sphere of the infinitude of consciousness**. After mastering Mudita, ask yourself, *"Is my consciousness existing in this infinity, or is this infinity existing in my consciousness?"* This contemplation leads to a profound understanding and concentration in the **second arupa jhana** (the sphere of infinite consciousness).

### 4. Equanimity (Upekkha) Meditation

**Transition from Mudita to Upekkha**

As Mudita fades, it transforms into a more tranquil and balanced state—**equanimity** (Upekkha). Upekkha is the ability to remain stable and composed in the face of all emotional extremes, neither overly joyful nor sorrowful.

- **Radiating Equanimity**

Radiate this feeling of calmness and balance in all

directions, starting with one and expanding to all six. Over time, you will naturally enter into the state of **equanimity absorption**, where the mind becomes deeply peaceful and still.

- **Attaining the Sphere of Infinite Nothingness**

  Upekkha meditation reaches its peak with the attainment of the **sphere of the infinitude of nothingness**. After practicing Upekkha for two hours, pay your attention to inwards, and contemplate the **nothingness** of all phenomena. This realization of emptiness leads to the **third arupa jhana**.

**Final Attainment: Neither Perception nor Non-Perception**

**Entering the Final Jhana**

Once in the sphere of nothingness, the mind may spontaneously enter the **fourth arupa jhana**, also known as the **sphere of neither-perception-nor non-perception.** In this state, the mind is so subtle that it cannot even perceive itself. It is akin to a dream-like state where the boundaries of consciousness blur, and the practitioner is aware but not fully cognizant of their awareness. This stage is marked by deep stillness and subtle, disconnected thoughts or images that arise and pass without any attachment or engagement.

- **Observing the Mind**

After emerging from the dream-like state, the mind becomes deeply alert, calm, and awake. You may feel a surge of energy, yet it is balanced, grounded energy. The key is to remain relaxed the moment you notice any movement or arising within the mind. Gradually, you will reach a state of complete disenchantment.

At this point, the mind can remain still for extended periods. You are delicately balancing the awakening factors—relaxation and focus—allowing the mind to rest in stillness. You might even experience brief moments of cessation, where the mind momentarily touches the state of cessation without fully stopping. These are all positive signs—simply continue observing.

Eventually, the mind will grow dispassionate towards all phenomena as they arise. You come to understand that these phenomena will never cease, and any attempt to control them is futile. The need to interfere dissolves, as you realize there is no controller. You stop trying to engage with everything, seeing that you cannot. As this understanding deepens, you may notice a sensation of the mind sinking, signifying the full experience of dispassion and the entry into pure emptiness.

- **Insight Concentration (Vipassana Samadhi)/ Emptiness**

  Emptiness is the state of pure, objectless awareness, where the mind is no longer focused on anything specific. When a vibration or sensation arises, the simple act of noticing it causes it to dissolve. In this space, there is no need to try to relax or engage with the vibration; just observing it is enough. Any attempt to interact with it beyond mere observation only creates further movement in the mind.

  The key is to let the vibration cease naturally, without interference—simply watching it pass. You adopt the mindset of, "I don't mind what arises; I will just let it pass on its own." It is here that the sense of "I," "myself," and "me" is revealed for what it is—a fleeting thought. This thought, known as conceit, is a form of craving, which brings discomfort. But in seeing it clearly, you let go of the attachment to "me" and free yourself from the suffering it creates.

- **Liberation/ Nibbana**

  Nibbāna, or liberation, is the profound state where all mental formations come to a complete halt. In this state of deep dispassion, the mind rests in profound stillness. At a certain moment, often when least expected, the entire flow of mental activity ceases. All perception, feeling, and consciousness dissolve into a state of total cessation—beyond all conditioned experiences.

This cessation signifies the realization of Nibbāna, where all preparatory mental activities are stilled. If this cessation does not occur spontaneously, you can further deepen your practice by relinquishing the sense of emptiness itself. Reflect on the nature of emptiness as impermanent and devoid of self. By doing so, you will enhance your experience of stilling all mental preparations, reaching the ultimate state of liberation.

**Conclusion**

The Brahma-Vihara meditations—*Metta, Karuna, Mudita,* and *Upekkha*—offer a profound and systematic path towards the cultivation of divine qualities and the stilling of the mind. These practices, when pursued diligently, lead to the mastery of higher concentration levels, from material *jhanas* to the formless *arupa jhanas*. They culminate in the ultimate experience of *Nibbana*, the cessation of all suffering. Through these meditative practices, the mind transcends its ordinary states, entering a divine abode, and ultimately, the realm of liberation.

# 33
# Attaining Jhana Through Ānāpānasati (Mindfulness of Breath)

In the practice of meditation, attaining the state of jhana, or deep meditative absorption, can be profoundly facilitated through the method of Anapanasati, or mindfulness of breath. This practice utilizes the breath as an anchor, guiding the meditator towards the various jhana factors that contribute to the experience of deep concentration and profound states of inner peace. The key to entering jhana lies in cultivating and refining these jhana factors, which are essential elements that, when developed, lead to the attainment of jhana. These factors include:

1. **Initial Application (Vitakka)**
2. **Sustained Application (Vicara)**
3. **Rapture (Píti)**
4. **Happiness (Sukha)**
5. **One-Pointedness (Ekaggata)**

Understanding and applying these factors within the context of Anapanasati can lead to a rich and profound meditative experience. Firstly, you should sit with straight spine and close your eyes as in previous meditations. Here is a detailed guide on how to approach and practice these stages:

**Step 1: Understanding the Long Breath**
Begin by focusing your attention on the breath. As you inhale, observe whether the breath is long. Recognize and mentally note, "I am breathing in long." This step is about simply acknowledging the length of the breath without any judgement or additional interpretation. This practice of discerning the breath's length is foundational for cultivating concentration.

**Step 2: Understanding the Short Breath**
As you exhale, determine if the breath is short. Label it accordingly with the awareness, "I am breathing out short." Just as a carpenter measures the length of each stroke before starting, you should recognize whether each breath is long or short from the beginning of the inhale or exhale. This helps in developing a detailed awareness of the breath.

**Step 3: Experiencing the Whole Body with the Breath**
Extend your awareness to include the entire body as you breathe in. Observe how the breath moves and permeates through the body. Similarly, as you breathe out, experience how the breath exits the body. This step connects the breath with the bodily sensations, fostering a

comprehensive awareness that integrates the breath with the entire physical experience.

**Step 4: Tranquillising the Breath**
Focus on calming the bodily sensations associated with the breath. As you inhale, train yourself to calm the physical sensations related to breathing, creating a sense of tranquility. Similarly, as you exhale, continue to calm these sensations. This step is crucial for achieving a state of calmness and serenity through the breath.

**Practicing the Jhana Factors**

Once you have established a stable mindfulness of the breath, you can begin to cultivate the jhana factors systematically. Follow these steps to develop and experience each jhana factor:

1. **Initial Application (Vitakka)**: Set a determination: "May I focus solely on the initial application for 10 minutes." During this time, pay close attention to the beginning of each breath, focusing on the initial application of awareness at the start of each inhale and exhale.
2. **Sustained Application (Vicara)**: After completing the initial application, set a determination: "May I focus solely on the sustained application for 10 minutes." Maintain your attention throughout the entire breath cycle, observing the full breath in and out, without losing focus.

3. **Rapture (Píti)**: Next, set a determination: "May I focus solely on the rapture for 10 minutes." Observe the joy and ecstasy that arise from paying attention to the breath. Allow yourself to experience the profound sense of delight that accompanies focused attention on the breath.
4. **Happiness (Sukha)**: Set a determination: "May I focus solely on happiness for 10 minutes." Notice the mental and physical pleasantness that arises with each breath. Allow this feeling of contentment to permeate your experience.
5. **One-Pointedness (Ekaggata)**: Finally, set a determination: "May I focus solely on one-pointedness for 10 minutes." Concentrate intensely on the breath, experiencing the unified state of mind that results from deep concentration.

**Combining the Jhana Factors**

Once you are comfortable with each factor individually, combine them progressively:

1. Set a determination: "May I experience the initial application and sustained application for 10 minutes." Practice integrating these two factors, observing how they work together.
2. Gradually add each factor: Continue by combining the initial application, sustained application, and rapture. Then, add happiness and one-pointedness sequentially.

3. Set a final determination: "May I experience all five jhana factors—initial application, sustained application, rapture, happiness, and one-pointedness—for 30 minutes." During this time, focus on incorporating all these factors into each breath, leading to a profound sense of absorption into jhana.

**Deepening the Jhana Practice**

Once you have attained the initial jhana, continue to practice and refine your experience:

1. **First Jhana**: Determine: "May I absorb into the first jhana and emerge after 15 minutes." Practice regularly, gradually extending the duration to 30 minutes, 1 hour, 2 hours, and shortening to 5 minutes, 2 minutes, one minute and 30 seconds, until you can sustain the first jhana state comfortably. Then discern 5 Jhana factors in detail one by one in the very time you emerge from the absorption. Note that you may initially find the initial application and sustained application to be somewhat rough, while the rapture, happiness, and one-pointedness will feel more peaceful and excellent.

2. **Second Jhana**: Set a determination: "May I absorb into the second jhana and emerge after 15 minutes." Focus on experiencing only the rapture,

happiness, and one-pointedness in each breath. Then you will absorb into the Jhana soon. Practice mastering this state for varying durations, eventually extending to 2 hours and reducing to 30 seconds as needed.

3. **Third Jhana**: Once you are comfortable with the second jhana, determine: "May I absorb into the third jhana and emerge after 15 minutes." Then focus on experiencing only the happiness, and one-pointedness in each breath in and breath out. Then you will absorb into the Jhana unintentionally. Here, you will discern that the rapture is somewhat rough, while only happiness and one-pointedness remain peaceful and excellent. Master this state for varying durations as before.

4. **Fourth Jhana**: Finally you will feel even happiness is also rough, but equanimity and one-pointedness is exceptionally peaceful and excellent. Then set a determination: "May I absorb into the fourth jhana and emerge after 15 minutes." Master this state in a similar manner, adjusting the duration as needed.

By following these detailed steps and systematically cultivating the jhana factors through mindfulness of breath, you can attain deeper states of jhana and refine your meditative practice.

# 34
# How to Insight into Jhana and Attain Liberation

Attaining jhana—profound states of meditative absorption—is a significant achievement in Buddhist meditation. However, to move beyond the states of jhana and achieve ultimate liberation, one must deeply understand and insight into the nature of these states. According to the *Jhana Nissaya Sutta* in the *Anguttara Nikaya* (Book of the Nines), this process involves a systematic examination and relinquishing of the five clinging aggregates through eleven distinct aspects. This approach helps in discerning the impermanent, unsatisfactory, and non-self nature of all phenomena, leading to the realization of emptiness and, ultimately, liberation.

## Understanding and Relinquishing the Five Clinging Aggregates

Upon emerging from any jhana state, the meditator should engage in a detailed contemplation of the five clinging aggregates, which are the components of experience that are habitually clung to and thus lead to suffering. These aggregates include:

1. **Form (Rupa)**
2. **Feeling or Sensation (Vedana)**
3. **Perception (Sanna)**
4. **Volitional Activities (Sankhara)**
5. **Consciousness (Vinnana)**

The following steps outline how to insightfully discern and relinquish each aggregate, fostering the progression towards liberation:

### 1. Discerning the Form (Body)

After emerging from the first jhana, contemplate the bodily form you experienced in the jhana. Note the following aspects:

- **Inconstant**: Recognize that the bodily sensations felt in jhana are subject to change.
- **Stressful**: Observe the stress and dissatisfaction inherent in the bodily form, even in the state of jhana.

- **A Disease**: Consider the body as a form of disease, causing discomfort and trouble.
- **An Abscess**: Understand that the form can be seen as an affliction or abscess, a source of suffering.
- **An Arrow**: See the body as an arrow piercing through, symbolizing the pain and suffering associated with physical existence.
- **A Curse**: Reflect on the body as a curse, trapping you in cycles of craving and dissatisfaction.
- **An Affliction**: Recognize the form as an ongoing affliction or burden.
- **Alien**: View the body as something foreign or alien, not intrinsically yours.
- **Disintegration**: Acknowledge that the body is subject to disintegration and decay.
- **Emptiness**: Contemplate the body as ultimately empty of inherent essence or self.
- **Not-Self**: Understand that the body, like all phenomena, is not a permanent self.

By discerning these aspects, relinquish the body from the mind. Recognize it as transient and not to be clung to.

### 2. Discerning Sensations

Next, apply the same contemplative process to the sensations (feelings) experienced in jhana:

- **Inconstant**: Sensations are fleeting and changeable.
- **Stressful**: Sensations often lead to stress and discomfort.

- **A Disease**: Sensations can be seen as a disease, causing distress and suffering.
- **An Abscess**: Sensations, like a wound, are sources of pain.
- **An Arrow**: Sensations can pierce and create discomfort.
- **A Curse**: Sensations can feel like a curse, trapping you in cycles of craving.
- **An Affliction**: Sensations can be an ongoing source of suffering.
- **Alien**: Consider sensations as foreign, not part of the true self.
- **Disintegration**: Recognize that sensations are subject to disintegration.
- **Emptiness**: See sensations as ultimately empty of self-nature.
- **Not-Self**: Understand that sensations are not a permanent self.

Relinquish the sensations from the mind by acknowledging their impermanent and non-self nature.

### 3. Discerning Perception

Apply the eleven aspects to perceptions, which are the mental formations that interpret sensory inputs:

- **Inconstant**: Perceptions are constantly changing.
- **Stressful**: Perceptions can be a source of mental stress.

- **A Disease**: Perceptions can lead to mental suffering and confusion.
- **An Abscess**: Perceptions can be like an affliction, causing discomfort.
- **An Arrow**: Perceptions can pierce and create mental distress.
- **A Curse**: Perceptions can trap the mind in cycles of craving and delusion.
- **An Affliction**: Perceptions can be an ongoing source of mental disturbance.
- **Alien**: View perceptions as foreign to the true nature of self.
- **Disintegration**: Perceptions are subject to disintegration.
- **Emptiness**: Recognize that perceptions are ultimately empty of inherent essence.
- **Not-Self**: Understand that perceptions are not a permanent self.

By discerning these qualities, relinquish perceptions from the mind.

### 4. Discerning Volitional Activities

Next, turn your attention to volitional activities (mental formations or intentions):

- **Inconstant**: Recognize that volitional activities are subject to change.
- **Stressful**: Volitional activities can create stress and dissatisfaction.

- **A Disease**: These activities can be like a disease, leading to mental suffering.
- **An Abscess**: They can cause affliction and trouble.
- **An Arrow**: They can pierce and create mental anguish.
- **A Curse**: Volitional activities can be seen as a curse, leading to ongoing dissatisfaction.
- **An Affliction**: They can be an ongoing source of mental affliction.
- **Alien**: View these activities as foreign to the true self.
- **Disintegration**: Recognize that they are subject to disintegration.
- **Emptiness**: Understand that volitional activities are ultimately empty of inherent self.
- **Not-Self**: Recognize that volitional activities are not a permanent self.

Relinquish these activities from the mind, understanding their transient and non-self nature.

### 5. Discerning Consciousness

Finally, apply the eleven aspects to consciousness:

- **Inconstant**: Consciousness is constantly changing.
- **Stressful**: Consciousness can be a source of mental stress.
- **A Disease**: Consciousness can lead to suffering and discomfort.

- **An Abscess**: It can be seen as an affliction, causing distress.
- **An Arrow**: Consciousness can create mental pain and suffering.
- **A Curse**: It can trap you in cycles of craving and dissatisfaction.
- **An Affliction**: Consciousness can be a continuous source of mental disturbance.
- **Alien**: View consciousness as foreign to the true self.
- **Disintegration**: Consciousness is subject to disintegration.
- **Emptiness**: Recognize consciousness as ultimately empty of inherent self.
- **Not-Self**: Understand that consciousness is not a permanent self.

Relinquish consciousness from the mind, acknowledging its impermanent and non-self nature.

**Experiencing Emptiness and Liberation**

Once you have relinquished these five aggregates from the mind, the state of emptiness—where all conditioned states cease except the observer. If emptiness does not arise automatically, apply a focused and quick discerning of these five aggregates and relinquish them into 5 sides. And pay particular attention to the central, then you will experience the emptiness.

By recognizing that even the state of emptiness is impermanent and not-self, you will come to a profound realization. Contemplate deeply: "This emptiness, too, is a preparation. There is a state even beyond this emptiness, which is more peaceful and excellent." Focus your attention beyond the state of emptiness to this transcendent level. Through such contemplation, you can attain Nibbana through the understanding of emptiness.

The realization of this state of liberation is marked by the profound peace and excellence of having transcended all conditioned phenomena. Through such insight and discernment, one attains the ultimate liberation, free from the cycles of craving and suffering.

# 35
# Implementing the Path of Liberation: *A Practical Guide*

To embark on and effectively implement the path to liberation, it is essential to establish a solid foundation rooted in faith, ethical conduct, and disciplined practice. Here's a comprehensive guide on how to proceed:

1. **Cultivate Faith in the Three Jewels**

The first and foremost step is to nurture unwavering faith in the Three Jewels: the Lord Buddha, the Dhamma (the teachings), and the Sangha (the community of practitioners and teachers). This faith acts as a guiding light on your journey to liberation, providing inspiration and motivation. Recognize and honor the Buddha as the enlightened teacher who has shown the path, the Dhamma as the profound teachings that guide you, and the Sangha as the supportive community that aids you in your practice.

**2. Adhere to the Five Precepts**

A critical aspect of the path is to observe the Five Precepts diligently. These precepts are:

- **Refrain from taking life**: Respect all living beings and refrain from harming them.
- **Refrain from taking what is not given**: Honor others' possessions and avoid theft or deceit.
- **Refrain from sexual misconduct**: Maintain ethical conduct in your relationships.
- **Refrain from false speech**: Practice truthfulness and avoid lying, gossip, and harsh speech.
- **Refrain from intoxicants**: Avoid substances that cloud the mind and lead to heedlessness.

Following these precepts helps to create a strong moral foundation that supports and enhances your meditation practice.

**3. Commit to Regular Meditation Practice**

Establish a regular meditation routine, aiming to meditate twice a day, each session lasting about 30 minutes. Utilize the meditation techniques outlined in this book to develop your concentration, insight, and understanding. Consistency in practice is key to deepening your meditation experience and advancing on the path to liberation.

**4. Engage with the Teachings Frequently**

Make it a habit to read this book regularly. Frequent engagement with the teachings reinforces your understanding and helps to integrate the concepts into your daily life. Revisit the material to deepen your insights and keep your practice aligned with the path to liberation.

5. **Seek Guidance from a Qualified Meditation Master**

Finding a skilled meditation master who can guide you is crucial. A qualified teacher can provide personalized instruction, offer valuable insights, and help you navigate challenges on your path. It's beneficial to seek out someone who can offer direct guidance and support.

6. **Join Our Online Meditation Programs**

For those seeking additional support and community, we offer online meditation programs conducted in English. Joining our meditation group allows you to participate in guided sessions every morning and evening, accommodating various time zones. Engaging in these group sessions can enhance your practice and provide a sense of belonging.

To learn more about our online meditation programs and join our community, visit www.venerableananda.org. For inquiries, you can email us at venerableananda@gmail.com or contact us via WhatsApp at +94-72-444-8-555. Additionally, for further insights and teachings, you can visit our YouTube channel: "Venerable Ananda."

### 7. Learn More About the Author

For further context and understanding, you can read more about the author in the introduction section of this book. Understanding the background and experience of the author can offer additional insights into the teachings and practices presented.

By following these steps with dedication and sincerity, you will be well on your way to implementing the path of liberation, advancing towards spiritual freedom, and experiencing profound inner peace.

***May all beings be happy, may all beings be free from suffering, may all beings realize the truth of non-self!***

**The End.**

***"Etadatthā, bhikkhave, kathā; etadatthā mantanā; etadatthā upanisā; etadatthaṃ sotāvadhānaṃ, yadidaṃ anupādā cittassa vimokkho."***

"Monks, that's the purpose of discussion, that's the purpose of counsel, that's the purpose of drawing near, that's the purpose of lending ear: for the liberation of the mind through no clinging."

**- Lord Buddha -**

www.ingramcontent.com/pod-product-compliance
Lightning Source LLC
Chambersburg PA
CBHW041738030726
47636CB00008B/490

* 9 7 8 1 0 3 6 9 0 0 5 7 1 *